THE PRESERVER'S HANDBOOK

YOUR ESSENTIAL GUIDE TO CANNING, PRESERVING, FERMENTING, FREEZING, AND DEHYDRATING FOR LONG-TERM STORAGE

KENT JAMESON

Published by:
Kent Jameson Publishing
16394 West Hilton Avenue
Goodyear, AZ 85338
kentjamesonpublishing@gmail.com
Printed in the United States of America.
First Printing, 2024
Library of Congress Cataloging-in-Publication Data:
Kent Jameson
The Preserver's Handbook: Your Essential Guide to Canning, Preserving, Fermenting, Freezing, and Dehydrating for Long-Term Storage.

TABLE OF CONTENTS

INTRODUCTION

As a young boy growing up in a small farm town in Iowa, I have vivid memories of summer days spent in my grandmother's kitchen. The air was always heavy with the rich aroma of ripe tomatoes, fresh-picked herbs, and the sweet fragrance of home-made jam. My grandmother would spend hours canning the fruits and vegetables that my grandfather nurtured in their garden. She wasn't just preserving food; she was preserving stories, memories, and a way of life that grounded us in the land and in each other. Some of my favorite memories are of fishing with my grandfather, knowing that the fish would later be worked into the soil to enrich the garden he cared for so deeply.

Those days ignited a passion in me for food preservation that has stayed with me ever since. I saw the magic in turning fresh produce into jars of goodness that could be enjoyed throughout the year. This passion has driven me to share the time-honored techniques of preserving food with others who seek to live healthier, more sustainable lives.

Today, many people face significant challenges when it comes to food. We have become heavily reliant on store-bought goods, which can be expensive and full of preservatives. Emergencies can disrupt our food supply, leaving us vulnerable. There is also a growing desire among people to take control of their food sources, ensuring what they eat is wholesome and free from harmful additives.

"The Preserver's Handbook" offers practical solutions to these problems. It is your guide to canning, preserving, fermenting, freezing, and dehydrating food for long-term storage. This book provides clear, step-by-step instructions that make it easy for anyone to start preserving food at home. You will find detailed guidance on food safety, ensuring that you can confidently store your preserved foods without worry.

What sets this book apart is its thoroughness and diversity of methods. You won't just learn one way to preserve food; you'll explore a variety of techniques, each with its own benefits. Whether you're a beginner or looking to refine your skills, this book covers it all. The focus on food safety is paramount, and the instructions are designed to be beginner-friendly while also offering advanced tips for those more experienced.

This book is for several types of readers. Preppers will find it invaluable for building a reliable food supply for uncertain times. Health-conscious individuals will appreciate the control it offers over ingredients, allowing them to reduce preservatives and additives in their diet. Culinary enthusiasts will discover a treasure trove of recipes and methods to enhance their cooking. Budget-conscious readers will see how preserving food can save money and reduce waste.

Food preservation offers numerous benefits. It allows you to enjoy seasonal produce all year round, ensuring a constant supply of nutritious food. It helps you save money by buying in bulk and reducing food waste. It provides a sense of self-sufficiency, knowing you have a stocked pantry. And it offers peace of mind, knowing you are prepared for emergencies.

In this book, you'll learn various methods of food preservation. We will cover water bath canning, pressure canning, dehydrating, freezing, and fermenting. Each method will be explained in detail, with step-by-step instructions to guide you through the process. You'll also find tips on equipment selection, storage space solutions, and a diverse selection of recipes, including meals in a jar.

Allow me to introduce myself. My name is Kent Jameson, and I hold a Bachelor of Science degree in Family and Consumer Sciences Journalism from Iowa State University. My upbringing in rural Iowa has given me a deep appreciation for the simplicity and wisdom of traditional practices. I have spent my life exploring the intersection of family, health, and everyday issues. My passion for natural health, alternative medicines, and sustainable living has led me to write this book. I want to share with you the knowledge and experience I have gained over the years.

I invite you to join me on this journey of food preservation. Whether you're looking to reduce your dependency on store-bought goods, prepare for emergencies, or simply enjoy healthier, preservative-free food, this book will provide you with all the tools and knowledge you need. Let's get started on this rewarding adventure together. Your pantry will thank you.

CHAPTER 1
GETTING STARTED WITH
FOOD PRESERVATION

One summer, after my grandparents had passed, I found myself in their old basement. The sun streamed through the small windows, casting a warm glow on the worn wooden shelving. On them were rows of jars filled with vibrant jams, pickles, and sauces. Each jar was a testament to their skill and love for preserving the bounty of their garden. It was then that I realized the true value of those jars—they represented not just food, but a legacy of self-sufficiency, preparedness, and health. This realization spurred me to dive deeper into the world of food preservation, a journey that has enriched my life in countless ways.

1.1 UNDERSTANDING FOOD PRESERVATION: WHY AND HOW

Food preservation has become increasingly important in modern times for a variety of reasons. For many, the desire to achieve self-sufficiency and reduce dependency on store-bought goods is a significant motivator. The idea of having a well-stocked pantry filled with home-preserved foods offers peace of mind, especially in times of uncertainty. Emergencies, whether natural disasters or economic crises, can disrupt food supplies, making long-term storage a practical and necessary solution.

Moreover, preserving food at home can lead to substantial cost savings. By buying in bulk or growing your own produce, you can reduce your grocery bills and make the most of seasonal abundance. Health-conscious individuals also find great value in food preservation, as it allows them to avoid the preservatives and additives commonly found in commercial products. Knowing exactly what goes into your food and controlling the ingredients gives you the confidence that you are consuming wholesome, natural products.

The basic principles of food preservation are rooted in science and practicality. Each method has its own unique process and rationale. Water bath canning, for instance, is suitable for high-acid foods such as fruits, pickles, and tomatoes. This method involves submerging jars in boiling water to create a vacuum seal, preventing spoilage. On the other hand, pressure canning is necessary for low-acid foods like vegetables, meats, and soups. It uses pressurized steam to reach higher temperatures, effectively killing harmful bacteria and ensuring long-term safety.

Dehydrating is another effective method, which involves removing moisture from foods to inhibit microbial growth. This method is perfect for fruits, vegetables, and even meats, transforming them into lightweight, shelf-stable snacks. Freezing, a method many are familiar with, slows down enzyme activity and microbial growth by keeping foods at a low temperature. It's a versatile technique suitable for a wide range of foods, from berries to steaks. Lastly, fermenting uses beneficial bacteria to preserve and enhance flavors in foods like sauerkraut, kimchi, and yogurt. This method not only extends shelf life but also boosts nutritional value through the production of probiotics.

Each preservation method offers distinct benefits. Longevity and shelf-stability are perhaps the most obvious. Properly canned, dehydrated, frozen, or fermented foods can last for months, even years, reducing the need for frequent grocery trips and ensuring you always have a supply of food on hand. Nutritional preservation and enhancement are additional benefits. Many methods, like fermenting, actually increase the nutritional content of foods. Dehydrating retains most of the vitamins and minerals, while freezing preserves the freshness and flavor of produce.

Versatility in recipes and uses is another significant advantage. Preserved foods can be used in a variety of dishes, from simple snacks to complex gourmet meals. They offer convenience and flexibility, allowing you to enjoy the flavors of summer in the dead of winter or whip up a quick meal with pantry staples.

Despite these clear benefits, there are common misconceptions about food preservation that can deter people from trying it. Some believe that canning is too difficult, but with beginner-friendly techniques and step-by-step instructions, anyone can learn to can successfully. Others worry that preserving food is unsafe. However, by following proper safety guidelines and tested recipes, you can confidently preserve food without fear of spoilage or contamination.

1.2 ESSENTIAL TOOLS AND EQUIPMENT FOR BEGINNERS

Embarking on the path of food preservation, you'll find that having the right tools can make all the difference. To start with, a water bath canner is indispensable for preserving high-acid foods like fruits and pickles. This tool uses boiling water to seal jars, effectively killing bacteria that could spoil the food. On the other hand, a pressure canner is crucial for low-acid foods such as vegetables and meats. By using pressurized steam, it reaches higher temperatures necessary to kill more resilient bacteria and ensure safe storage.

A good dehydrator is another essential piece of equipment. It removes moisture from foods, which inhibits microbial growth and extends shelf life. Look for models with adjustable temperature settings and good airflow design to ensure even drying. Freezer-safe containers are equally important for those who prefer freezing their produce. These containers should be airtight to prevent freezer burn and maintain the quality of the food. For those interested in fermenting, a fermentation crock or jars with airlocks are highly recommended. These tools help create the anaerobic environment needed for beneficial bacteria to thrive and preserve the food.

When selecting quality equipment, there are several factors to consider. Durability and safety certifications are paramount. Equipment should be built to last and meet safety standards to avoid any risks associated with food preservation. Size and capacity are also critical. Depending on how much food you plan to preserve, choose equipment that can handle your needs without being overly cumbersome. Versatility is another key aspect. Multifunctional tools that can be used for various preservation methods can save you both space and money.

Budget-friendly options are available for those who may find specialized equipment too costly. For water bath canning, a large stockpot with a fitted lid can often serve the purpose. Just ensure it's deep enough to cover the jars with water. DIY dehydrating methods, such as using an oven on a low setting, can be effective if you don't have a dehydrator. Repurposing jars and containers you already have can also be a cost-saving measure. Just make sure they are suitable for the type of preservation you're doing.

Maintaining and caring for your equipment is crucial for longevity and safety. Proper cleaning and storage are the first steps. Always clean your tools thoroughly after each use and store them in a dry place to prevent rust and deterioration. Regularly inspect your equipment for wear and tear. Look for cracks in jars, worn gaskets in canners, and any signs of damage in your dehydrator. Calibration and safety checks for canners are particularly important. Ensure that pressure gauges are accurate and that safety valves function correctly. This ensures that your food will be processed safely and effectively.

Take the time to understand each piece of equipment and its maintenance needs. For instance, pressure canners often require annual testing of their gauges to ensure accuracy. Many local extension offices offer this service for free or at a low cost. Dehydrators with removable trays and components should be disassembled and cleaned regularly to remove food particles that could harbor bacteria. Fermentation crocks and jars should be scrubbed clean and thoroughly dried before storing to prevent mold growth.

By investing in the right tools and learning how to maintain them, you set yourself up for success in food preservation. You'll find that the initial investment pays off in the long run through the consistent quality and safety of your preserved foods. Whether you're canning, dehydrating, freezing, or fermenting, having reliable equipment will make the process smoother and more enjoyable. Remember, quality tools can be the difference between a successful preservation season and a frustrating one. Equip yourself well, and you'll be ready to tackle any preservation project with confidence.

1.3 FOOD SAFETY 101: AVOIDING SPOILAGE AND CONTAMINATION

Ensuring food safety in preservation is paramount. Understanding acidity levels is crucial for canning. High-acid foods, like fruits and pickles, have a pH below 4.6, making them suitable for water bath canning. This acidity inhibits the growth of harmful bacteria, ensuring safe storage. On the other hand, low-acid foods, like vegetables and meats, require pressure canning. This method uses high heat and pressure to kill bacteria and spores, such as Clostridium botulinum, which can cause botulism—a severe form of food poisoning. Recognizing these distinctions helps in choosing the correct method for each type of food.

Sterilization and cleanliness play a critical role in food safety. Before starting any preservation process, ensure all equipment and surfaces are thoroughly cleaned. Sterilizing jars and lids in boiling water for at least ten minutes eliminates bacteria and other microorganisms that could spoil the food. Regularly washing hands and using clean utensils further reduces the risk of contamination. Recognizing signs of spoilage is also essential. Spoiled food may exhibit changes in color, odor, or texture. Bulging lids, leaking jars, or off-smells are clear indicators that the food is no longer safe to eat.

Safe canning practices involve several key steps. First, maintaining proper headspace in jars is vital. This space allows for food expansion during processing and helps create a vacuum seal. Too little headspace can cause the food to overflow, while too much can prevent a proper seal. Secondly, sealing techniques are crucial. After filling jars, wipe the rims clean and place the lid on top. Screw the band on fingertip tight to secure the lid without over-tightening. Processing times and pressure adjustments based on altitude are also critical. Higher altitudes require longer processing times or increased pressure to ensure safety. Always refer to tested recipes and guidelines for accurate processing times.

When dehydrating and freezing foods, specific safety measures must be followed. Dehydrating requires maintaining safe temperatures. Most fruits and vegetables should be dried at 125°F to 135°F. Meats and fish should be dehydrated at 145°F to ensure they are safe to eat. Proper packaging is essential to prevent freezer burn when freezing foods. Use airtight containers or vacuum-sealed bags to maintain the quality of the food. Blanching vegetables before freezing is another important step. This process involves boiling vegetables briefly and then plunging them into ice water. Blanching stops enzyme activity, preserving the color, texture, and nutritional value of the vegetables.

Addressing common safety concerns is vital for successful food preservation. Botulism prevention in canning is a significant concern. Always use tested recipes and follow recommended processing times and pressures. Avoiding cross-contamination is another key aspect. Use separate cutting boards and utensils for raw and cooked foods. Clean surfaces and tools thoroughly between uses. Safe fermentation practices are also essential to prevent mold and spoilage. Use clean jars and weights to keep the food submerged in the brine, creating an anaerobic environment that supports beneficial bacteria while inhibiting harmful ones.

Incorporating these food safety principles into your preservation practices will ensure that your preserved foods are safe and enjoyable. By understanding the role of acidity, maintaining cleanliness, and following proper techniques, you can confidently preserve a wide variety of foods. Whether you are canning, dehydrating, freezing, or fermenting, adhering to these guidelines will help you avoid spoilage and contamination, ensuring that your preserved foods remain safe and delicious for long-term storage.

1.4 PREPARING YOUR KITCHEN FOR PRESERVATION SUCCESS

Setting up your kitchen for food preservation is crucial for ensuring both efficiency and safety. A well-organized space streamlines your workflow, minimizes contamination risks, and makes the entire process more enjoyable. Start by designating a clean, clutter-free area where you can work comfortably. This could be a section of your countertop or a dedicated table. Clear away any unnecessary items that could get in the way or introduce contaminants. Ensure your workspace is well-lit and ventilated. Good lighting helps you see what you're doing, while proper ventilation keeps the area cool and reduces the risk of spoilage.

Organizing your tools and equipment for accessibility is another key step. Store frequently used items within easy reach and keep lesser-used tools in nearby cabinets. Use drawer organizers and hooks to keep utensils, funnels, and jar lifters neatly arranged. Shelves can hold your canners, dehydrators, and fermentation crocks. Labeling shelves and drawers can also save time, especially when you're in the middle of a preservation project and need to find something quickly. Consider investing in a rolling cart for mobile storage, allowing you to move your tools around as needed.

Cleanliness and hygiene are paramount in food preservation. Regularly clean surfaces and tools to prevent contamination. Use food-safe cleaning agents and avoid harsh chemicals that could leave residues. Sanitize countertops, cutting boards, and utensils before and after each use. Pay special attention to areas where raw produce and meats are handled. A simple solution of water and white vinegar can be an effective disinfectant. Wash your hands thoroughly and frequently, especially when switching between different tasks. Keeping your workspace clean reduces the risk of foodborne illnesses and ensures that your preserved foods remain safe to eat.

Managing space and storage efficiently can make a world of difference, especially in smaller kitchens. Utilize vertical storage and shelving to maximize your available space. Install wall-mounted racks for storing jars and equipment. Stackable containers can help you organize ingredients and utensils. Multi-purpose tools can also save space. For instance, a food processor with multiple attachments can handle slicing, dicing, and pureeing, eliminating the need for separate gadgets. Think creatively about your storage solutions. Even a small kitchen can be optimized to support your food preservation efforts with the right organization.

Time-saving practices are invaluable for busy preservers. Batch processing and meal prepping can significantly reduce the time you spend on food preservation. Set aside specific days for different tasks, such as washing and prepping produce one day, and canning or dehydrating the next. This approach helps you stay organized and focused. Efficient jar sterilization methods, like using a dishwasher with a sanitize cycle, can save time. Pre-cutting and organizing ingredients before you start the preservation process can also streamline your workflow. Having everything prepped and ready to go minimizes interruptions and helps you work more efficiently.

A clean, organized, and well-equipped workspace not only stream-lines the process but also guarantees that your preserved foods are safe and of the highest quality. By integrating these strategies into your kitchen setup, you'll create an environment that fosters successful food preservation. Whether you're just starting out or seeking to enhance your current setup, these tips will help you maximize your kitchen's potential. By investing time in properly preparing your space, you'll set the stage for success in all your preservation efforts.

1.5 INGREDIENT SOURCING: FINDING QUALITY PRODUCE AND MEATS

The foundation of successful food preservation lies in the quality of your ingredients. Freshness and ripeness are paramount because the better the starting material, the better the preserved product will be. Fresh, ripe produce not only tastes better but also retains more nutrients. For instance, a ripe tomato from a local farm will have a fuller flavor and higher nutritional content compared to one that has been sitting on a supermarket shelf for days. Similarly, when it comes to meats, the quality of the cut directly affects the texture and taste after preservation. Opting for lean cuts ensures that the meat doesn't turn rancid quickly, while selecting well-marbled cuts can add flavor but requires careful handling to avoid spoilage.

The debate between organic and conventional produce often arises when sourcing ingredients. Organic produce is grown without synthetic pesticides or fertilizers, making it a healthier choice for many. However, it can be more expensive and sometimes harder to find. Conventional produce, while more affordable and accessible, may contain pesticide residues. If possible, prioritize organic for items you consume regularly or those with high pesticide levels, like berries or leafy greens. However, the key is to select the freshest, highest quality produce you can afford, whether organic or conventional.

Finding quality ingredients locally and affordably is achievable with a bit of effort. Farmers' markets and local farms are excellent sources of fresh, seasonal produce. Shopping at these venues supports local agriculture and often results in better-tasting food. Additionally, forming relationships with local farmers can provide you with insights into the best times to buy and even lead to discounts on bulk purchases. Growing your own vegetables and herbs is another fantastic way to ensure a steady supply of fresh, organic produce. Even a small garden can yield a surprising amount of food, and you have complete control over how it's grown.

Bulk buying and seasonal shopping are practical strategies for sourcing ingredients affordably. Many farms offer bulk discounts during peak harvest times, allowing you to stock up when produce is at its best and most affordable. Seasonal shopping means buying fruits and vegetables when they are naturally abundant and cheaper. For example, buying strawberries in June when they are in season is both cost-effective and ensures the best flavor. Freezing or canning these seasonal treasures allows you to enjoy them year-round without paying the premium prices seen out of season.

When choosing meats for preservation, several factors need consideration. Lean cuts, such as chicken breasts, pork loins, and certain cuts of beef, are ideal because they have less fat, reducing the risk of rancidity. Free-range and grass-fed options are often higher in quality and better in flavor and nutrition. These meats come from animals that have been raised in more natural environments, resulting in healthier, tastier products. Safe handling and preparation are crucial. Always ensure that meat is fresh, properly trimmed, and portioned before preservation. This includes removing excess fat, which can spoil faster and affect the overall quality of the preserved meat.

Preparing ingredients for preservation requires attention to detail. Start by thoroughly washing and peeling fruits and vegetables to remove dirt, bacteria, and pesticide residues. For instance, scrub root vegetables like carrots and potatoes under running water and peel if necessary. Trimming and portioning meats involves removing excess fat and cutting the meat into manageable pieces. For example, cut chicken breasts into strips if you plan to dehydrate them into jerky. Pre-treating certain foods, such as blanching vegetables, is also essential. Blanching involves briefly boiling vegetables and then plunging them into ice water. This process preserves color, texture, and nutritional value, making the final preserved product more appealing and nutritious.

Starting with high-quality ingredients and preparing them meticulously can make all the difference in your preservation efforts. Fresh, ripe produce and well-chosen meats not only taste better but also preserve more effectively. Local sourcing, bulk buying, and careful handling ensure that you get the best results from your preservation projects. By paying attention to these details, you'll find that the food you preserve is not only safe and long-lasting but also delicious and nutritious.

CHAPTER 2
WATER BATH CANNING
BASICS

2.1 INTRODUCTION TO WATER BATH CANNING

W ater bath canning is a fundamental technique in the world of food preservation, particularly suited for high-acid foods such as fruits, jams, jellies, and pickles. This method involves submerging jars filled with prepared food into a bath of boiling water. The high temperature effectively kills any microorganisms that could spoil the food, while the boiling process creates a vacuum seal as the jars cool down. This vacuum seal is crucial for preserving the food and preventing contamination. It's a method that has been trusted for generations due to its simplicity and effectiveness.

One of the primary reasons water bath canning is so popular is its accessibility. Unlike pressure canning, which requires specialized equipment, water bath canning only requires a large, deep pot with a lid and a rack. This makes it an ideal method for beginners who might be intimidated by the more complex procedures of pressure canning. The simplicity of this method allows anyone to start preserving their own food with minimal investment. You can use common kitchen items like a wooden spoon, ladle, and paring knife, making it a cost-effective way to begin your journey into food preservation.

Water bath canning is particularly effective for preserving high-acid foods. Fruits like apples, berries, and peaches are perfect candidates for this method. The natural acidity of these fruits, combined with the high temperatures of the boiling water, ensures that they can be safely preserved for long periods. Pickled vegetables are another excellent option. The vinegar used in the pickling process adds to the acidity, making them safe for water bath canning. Jams, jellies, and preserves are also ideally suited for this method. The sugar content in these spreads helps to preserve them, while the boiling water bath ensures they are safe to store and enjoy throughout the year.

However, it's important to understand the limitations of water bath canning. This method is not suitable for low-acid foods such as vegetables, meats, and soups. Low-acid foods require the higher temperatures that can only be achieved with a pressure canner to ensure safety. Using water bath canning for these foods could result in spoilage or even the risk of botulism, a serious and potentially fatal foodborne illness. Therefore, it's crucial to adhere to specific recipes and guidelines, ensuring that you only use water bath canning for foods that are safely preserved using this method.

While water bath canning is straightforward, it does require attention to detail. Following tested recipes is essential to ensure that you maintain the correct acidity levels and processing times. Always use the recommended amounts of acid ingredients like lemon juice or vinegar. These acids are critical for creating an environment that inhibits bacterial growth. Reducing or substituting these ingredients can compromise the safety of your preserved foods. Similarly, processing times must be followed precisely. Shortening the time can result in under processed jars, which can spoil or become unsafe to eat.

Water bath canning offers a wonderful way to preserve the flavors of summer and enjoy them throughout the year. Its simplicity and accessibility make it an excellent choice for beginners, while its effectiveness ensures that your preserved foods are safe and delicious. By understanding its appropriate applications and limitations, you can confidently use water bath canning to stock your pantry with a variety of high-acid foods. This method not only allows you to enjoy fresh, seasonal produce year-round but also provides a sense of accomplishment and self-sufficiency.

2.2 STEP-BY-STEP WATER BATH CANNING PROCESS

Water bath canning might seem a bit daunting at first, but once you break it down, it's a straightforward and rewarding process.

Prepare Your Food and Jars

Let's start by preparing your food and jars. Begin by washing your produce thoroughly under running water to remove any dirt or contaminants. If you're working with fruits, peeling and cutting them into uniform pieces ensures even cooking and better packing. For jams and jellies, follow your recipe to cook the fruit, sugar, and pectin together. While you're prepping your food, place your canning jars in a large pot of simmering water (around 180°F) to keep them hot. This step prevents the jars from breaking when filled with hot food.

Fill and Seal the Jars

Next, it's time to fill and seal the jars. Using a jar lifter, remove one jar from the hot water, carefully draining the water back into the pot. Place the jar on a clean towel to avoid thermal shock from a cold countertop. Use a canning funnel to fill the jar with your prepared food, leaving the recommended headspace as specified in your recipe. This space is crucial for ensuring a proper vacuum seal. For most foods, leaving a half inch of headspace is standard. Once filled, use a non-metallic utensil to remove any air bubbles by sliding it around the inside edges of the jar. Adjust the headspace if necessary. Wipe the rim of the jar with a clean, damp cloth to remove any food residue that could interfere with sealing. Place a lid on top, then screw on the band until it is fingertip tight.

Process the Jars

Now, let's move on to processing the jars in the water bath canner. Ensure your canning rack is at the bottom of the pot to keep jars from touching the bottom directly. Carefully lower the filled and sealed jars into the canner using the jar lifter. Add enough hot water to cover the jars by at least one to two inches. Place the lid on the canner and bring the water to a rolling boil. Start your timer once the water reaches a full boil. Processing times vary depending on the recipe and altitude, so always refer to your specific recipe for accurate timing. Maintaining a steady boil throughout the processing time is essential for ensuring the food is preserved safely.

Ensuring a successful seal is critical in water bath canning. One key aspect is maintaining proper headspace. Too much or too little can prevent jars from sealing correctly. Always follow your recipe's guidelines. Wiping the jar rims before sealing is another important step. Any residue left on the rim can prevent the lid from adhering properly, leading to a failed seal. Checking for air bubbles is also necessary. Trapped air can expand during processing, potentially breaking the seal or causing spoilage. Running a non-metallic utensil around the inside edge of the jar helps release any trapped air.

Turn Off Heat and Let Sit

Once the processing time is complete, turn off the heat and let the jars sit in the canner for an additional five minutes. This brief resting period helps stabilize the contents and prevent siphoning. Using the jar lifter, carefully remove each jar from the canner and place them on a towel-lined countertop. It's important to allow the jars to cool undisturbed for 12-24 hours. As they cool, you'll hear the satisfying "ping" of lids sealing, indicating a successful vacuum seal. Avoid touching or moving the jars during this cooling period to ensure a proper seal.

Test the Seals

After the jars have cooled, it's time to test the seals. Press the center of each lid with your finger. If the lid doesn't flex up and down, the jar is sealed correctly. If it does flex, the jar didn't seal properly and should be refrigerated and used within a few days.

Label and Store

Properly sealed jars should be labeled with the contents and date. Store them in a cool, dark, and dry place. A pantry or basement shelf works well. Proper labeling and storage help you keep track of your preserved foods and ensure they are used within their optimal time frame.

2.3 CHOOSING THE RIGHT JARS AND LIDS

Selecting the right jars and lids is a crucial aspect of water bath canning. The market offers a variety of options, including brands like Mason jars, Ball jars, and others. Each of these brands has its own set of features, but the fundamental choice often comes down to size and mouth type. Half-pint jars are ideal for jams and jellies, while pint and quart jars are better suited for preserving fruits and pickled vegetables. When choosing between regular and wide-mouth jars, consider the type of food you'll be canning. Wide-mouth jars are easier to fill and empty, making them perfect for larger chunks of fruit or pickles. Regular mouth jars, on the other hand, are more compact and take up less space, which can be an advantage when storage is limited.

Using proper lids and bands is essential for achieving a safe and effective seal. Most canning lids come in a two-piece set: a flat lid and a screw band. The flat lid has a sealing compound that adheres to the jar rim during the canning process, creating a vacuum seal as the jar cools. The screw band holds the lid in place during processing and can be reused multiple times, but the flat lids should be used only once. Reusing lids can compromise the seal, increasing the risk of spoilage. Always ensure that lids are free from rust and damage before use. Any imperfections can prevent a proper seal, rendering your preservation efforts ineffective.

Finding quality jars and lids can be straightforward if you know where to look. Trusted brands like Ball and Kerr are reliable choices, offering consistent quality and durability. Buying in bulk can save you money in the long run, especially if you plan to preserve large quantities of food. Many local stores carry canning supplies, but online retailers often offer a wider selection and the convenience of home delivery. When shopping in local stores, inspect the jars and lids for any signs of damage. Online reviews can also be helpful in determining the reliability of a product before making a purchase.

Maintenance and reuse of jars are equally important. Always start by cleaning and sterilizing your jars before use. This can be done by washing them in hot, soapy water and then boiling them for at least ten minutes. Inspect each jar for chips or cracks, as these can lead to breakage during the canning process. Lids and bands should also be cleaned thoroughly, and any rusted or bent bands should be discarded. Proper storage of lids and bands is essential to prevent damage. Store them in a dry, cool place, away from moisture and heat, which can degrade the sealing compound and metal.

In conclusion, choosing the right jars and lids involves understanding the different types available and their specific uses. Proper maintenance and storage ensure that your canning efforts are successful, and your preserved foods remain safe to eat. Knowing where to buy quality products and how to care for them will set you up for a smooth and efficient canning process. Whether you're a beginner or an experienced preserver, paying attention to these details can make a significant difference in the quality and safety of your canned goods.

2.4 COMMON MISTAKES AND HOW TO AVOID THEM

When it comes to water bath canning, even small mistakes can lead to significant problems. One of the most frequent errors is incorrect headspace. This often happens when jars are either overfilled or underfilled. Too little headspace can cause the food to expand and overflow during processing, while too much headspace can prevent the jar from sealing properly. Both scenarios can compromise the safety and quality of your preserved food. Another common mistake is improper sealing techniques. If the rims of the jars are not wiped clean before placing the lids, or if the bands are screwed on too tightly or too loosely, the jars might not seal correctly. Inadequate processing times are another issue. Not boiling the jars for the recommended time can result in under processed food, which is unsafe to eat.

To correct these mistakes, you can take several actionable steps. First, always use a non-metallic utensil to adjust the headspace. This tool helps you remove air bubbles and ensure the right amount of space is left at the top of the jar. Ensuring jars are fully submerged during processing is crucial. The water level should be at least one to two inches above the tops of the jars to ensure even heating. Following tested recipes is another vital step. These recipes have been designed with specific processing times and temperatures to ensure safety. Deviating from these guidelines can result in under processed food, which can spoil or become unsafe to eat.

The consequences of these common mistakes can be severe. Spoilage is the most immediate risk. If jars do not seal properly or are not processed for the correct amount of time, bacteria can grow inside, leading to spoiled food. This not only wastes your effort but can also be dangerous if consumed. Foodborne illnesses, such as botulism, are a serious risk if canning is not done correctly. Loss of vacuum seal is another issue. Without a proper vacuum seal, the food is exposed to air, which can lead to spoilage and altered taste and texture. The food may become mushy, discolored, or develop off-flavors, making it unappetizing and potentially unsafe.

Troubleshooting these issues requires a keen eye and some practical knowledge. If jars don't seal properly, the first step is to check the lids. If the center of the lid pops up and down when pressed, the jar hasn't sealed. In this case, you can reprocess the jar within 24 hours. Simply replace the lid and reprocess the jar for the full time specified in the recipe. Identifying signs of spoilage is crucial. Look for bulging lids, off smells, or any visible mold inside the jar. If you notice any of these signs, dispose of the jar immediately. Do not taste the contents, as they could be harmful. Correcting under processed jars involves reprocessing them. If you realize that jars were not boiled for the correct amount of time, you can reprocess them within 24 hours for the full time required.

Addressing these common mistakes and understanding their consequences ensures that your water bath canning efforts are both safe and successful. By paying attention to details like headspace, sealing techniques, and processing times, you can avoid the pitfalls that many beginners encounter. Troubleshooting issues as they arise and knowing how to correct them will give you the confidence to can a variety of high-acid foods successfully. This knowledge not only helps preserve the quality and safety of your food but also makes the canning process more enjoyable and rewarding.

In water bath canning, strict adherence to safety guidelines is non-negotiable. Following tested recipes, performing thorough safety checks, and recognizing signs of spoilage protect you and your loved ones from foodborne illnesses. Proper long-term storage ensures that your efforts in the kitchen translate into safe, nutritious, and tasty foods that can be enjoyed throughout the year. By mastering these safety practices, you not only preserve the bounty of your harvest but also contribute to a more self-sufficient and secure lifestyle.

CHAPTER 3
MASTERING PRESSURE CANNING

3.1 UNDERSTANDING PRESSURE CANNING: THE SCIENCE BEHIND IT

Pressure canning is a vital method for preserving low-acid foods safely. Unlike water bath canning, which relies on boiling water to create a vacuum seal, pressure canning uses pressurized steam to achieve much higher temperatures. This high temperature is crucial for destroying Clostridium botulinum spores, which can cause botulism—a severe form of food poisoning. The spores can survive boiling temperatures but are effectively killed at the 240°F to 250°F range achieved in a pressure canner. Maintaining the correct pressure throughout the canning process ensures that these temperatures are consistently reached, safeguarding the food from potential contamination.

Low-acid foods require pressure canning due to their higher pH levels, which can support the growth of harmful bacteria if not processed correctly. Vegetables such as green beans, carrots, and corn are prime examples of low-acid foods that must be pressure canned. Meats and poultry also fall into this category. Whether you're preserving chicken breasts, beef stew, or pork chops, pressure canning ensures these proteins are stored safely. Combination recipes like soups and stews, which often include a mix of low-acid vegetables and meats, also necessitate this method. The diverse ingredients in these recipes require the higher temperatures of pressure canning to ensure all components are safely preserved.

The distinction between pressure canning and boiling water bath canning is critical. Boiling water bath canning is suitable for high-acid foods, which have a pH level of 4.6 or lower. The natural acidity of these foods, combined with the boiling temperature of 212°F, is sufficient to prevent the growth of harmful bacteria. However, this method is inadequate for low-acid foods, which require the higher temperatures of pressure canning. The pressurized environment of a pressure canner allows water to reach temperatures up to 250°F, effectively destroying bacteria and spores that thrive in low-acid environments. Understanding the pH levels of the foods you intend to preserve is essential for choosing the appropriate canning method.

Following tested recipes is paramount in pressure canning. Reliable sources like the USDA's Complete Guide to Home Canning provide research-based recommendations that ensure safety and quality. These guidelines take into account the specific processing times and pressures needed to safely preserve different types of foods. Avoiding substitutions and modifications is crucial. Even seemingly minor changes, like altering the amount of vinegar in a recipe, can affect the acidity and compromise safety. The role of processing times and pressures cannot be overstated. Each recipe specifies the exact time and pressure required to achieve the necessary temperature for safe preservation. Adhering to these guidelines ensures that your preserved foods are safe to store and consume.

In summary, pressure canning is an indispensable method for preserving low-acid foods. By using pressurized steam to achieve high temperatures, it effectively destroys harmful bacteria and spores, ensuring long-term storage safety. Understanding the types of foods that require pressure canning and the science behind the process is essential. Adhering to tested recipes and guidelines ensures that your efforts result in safe, high-quality preserved foods. As you become more familiar with pressure canning, you'll find it to be a reliable and rewarding method for stocking your pantry with a diverse array of nutritious meals.

3.2 ESSENTIAL EQUIPMENT FOR PRESSURE CANNING

When it comes to pressure canning, having the right equipment is paramount. The centerpiece of your setup will be the pressure canner itself. There are two main types: dial-gauge and weighted-gauge canners. Dial-gauge canners have a gauge that shows the pressure inside the canner and require manual adjustment of the burner heat. This allows for precise control and is especially useful at higher altitudes where small pressure adjustments are needed. However, they require regular accuracy testing, typically once a year, to ensure the gauge is functioning correctly. Weighted-gauge canners, on the other hand, release excess pressure automatically and do not need accuracy testing. They are simpler to use but offer less flexibility in pressure adjustments, especially at altitudes above 1,000 feet where they typically jump from 10 lbs to 15 lbs pressure.

In addition to the pressure canner, you'll need canning jars, lids, and bands. Canning jars come in various sizes, from half-pint to quart, and choosing the right size depends on what you're preserving. Lids are usually one-time use, while the bands can be reused as long as they are in good condition. A jar lifter is an indispensable tool for safely moving hot jars in and out of the canner, and a funnel helps you fill jars without spills, keeping rims clean for a proper seal.

Maintaining your pressure canner is crucial for both safety and effectiveness. Annual gauge testing for accuracy is a must if you use a dial-gauge canner. Many local extension offices offer this service. Inspecting and replacing gaskets is another important step. Gaskets can wear out and develop cracks over time, compromising the seal and pressure inside the canner. Regularly check the gasket and replace it if you notice any signs of wear. Cleaning your canner after each use is essential. Remove any food particles and residue, and store the canner in a dry place to prevent rust and corrosion.

Several additional tools can enhance your pressure canning process. A bubble remover or headspace tool is invaluable for ensuring the correct headspace in your jars and removing trapped air bubbles. This simple tool helps prevent under processing and ensures a proper seal. A kitchen timer and thermometer are also useful. The timer helps you keep track of processing times accurately, while the thermometer can verify the internal temperature of your canner if needed. Racks and dividers for jar placement ensure that jars are not directly touching the bottom of the canner or each other, promoting even heat distribution and preventing breakage.

Understanding the differences between dial-gauge and weighted-gauge canners helps you choose the right equipment for your needs. Dial-gauge canners offer more precise pressure control but require regular calibration. They are ideal for those who live at varying altitudes and need to make small adjustments. Weighted-gauge canners are easier to use and maintain but offer less flexibility in pressure settings. They are a great option for beginners or those who prefer a more straightforward approach.

With the right equipment and proper maintenance, pressure canning becomes a safe and efficient way to preserve low-acid foods. Each tool plays a critical role, from the canner itself to the accessories that make the process smoother and more reliable. By investing in quality equipment and taking the time to care for it, you ensure successful canning results and a pantry stocked with safe, delicious preserved foods.

3.3 STEP-BY-STEP PRESSURE CANNING PROCESS

Prepare Your Food and Jars

Pressure canning starts with preparing both your food and jars meticulously. Begin by washing your produce or meats thoroughly. For vegetables, peel and cut them into uniform pieces to ensure even processing. Meats should be trimmed of excess fat and cut into portions that fit comfortably in your jars. Once your food is prepped, move on to the jars. Clean jars are crucial; wash them in hot, soapy water and rinse well. Place the jars in a pot of simmering water to keep them hot. This prevents thermal shock when you add hot food. While the jars are heating, prepare your lids according to the manufacturer's instructions, usually by simmering them in a small pot of water.

Fill and Seal the Jars/Load the Canner

Loading the canner and securing the lid is the next step. Using a jar lifter, remove one jar from the hot water, drain it, and place it on a clean towel. Use a funnel to fill the jar with your prepared food, leaving the recommended headspace, typically one inch for most low-acid foods. Adjust the headspace by adding or removing food as needed. Use a non-metallic utensil to remove air bubbles by sliding it around the inside of the jar. Wipe the rim clean with a damp cloth to ensure a good seal. Place a lid on the jar and screw the band on until it's fingertip tight. Load the filled jars into the canner, ensuring they are not touching each other. Add the required amount of water to the canner, usually about three quarts, but always check your canner's manual for specifics.

Building Pressure and Venting the Canner

Venting the canner and building pressure is a critical phase. Secure the canner lid according to the manufacturer's instructions, making sure it's locked in place. Turn the heat to high and wait for steam to start escaping from the vent pipe. This steam needs to be vented for ten minutes to ensure all air is expelled from the canner, which is crucial for building the correct pressure. After venting, place the pressure regulator on the vent pipe. The canner will start to pressurize, and the pressure gauge or weight will indicate when the desired pressure is reached. This is typically 10 or 15 pounds per square inch (psi), depending on your altitude and the food being canned.

Ensuring accurate pressure control throughout the canning process is vital. Monitor the pressure gauge or weight closely. If you're using a dial-gauge canner, adjust the heat to maintain a steady pressure. Too high, and you risk overcooking your food; too low, and you may not reach the necessary temperature to kill harmful bacteria. A weighted-gauge canner will jiggle to release excess pressure automatically, but you still need to keep an eye on it. Using a kitchen timer is essential for precise processing times. Start the timer only when the correct pressure is reached, and adjust the heat as needed to maintain that pressure throughout the processing time.

Depressurizing and Cooling

The cooling and storage process begins once the processing time is complete. Turn off the heat and allow the canner to depressurize naturally. Do not rush this step by removing the weight or opening the vent pipe, as this can cause the jars to siphon and lose liquid, compromising the seal. Once the pressure gauge reads zero, wait an additional ten minutes before removing the lid. Always open the lid away from you to avoid steam burns. Using a jar lifter, carefully remove the jars and place them on a towel-lined surface to cool undisturbed for 12-24 hours.

Test the Seals

Testing seals after cooling is straightforward. Press the center of each lid; if it doesn't flex, the jar is sealed. If a lid does flex, the jar didn't seal properly and should be refrigerated and used within a few days, or you can reprocess it within 24 hours.

Label and Store

Proper labeling is the next step. Use a permanent marker to write the contents and the date on each lid. Store your sealed jars in a cool, dark, and dry place. A pantry or basement shelf works well. Regularly check your stored jars for any signs of spoilage, such as bulging lids or leaks, and consume them within a year for the best quality.

3.4 TROUBLESHOOTING PRESSURE CANNING ISSUES

Pressure canning, while incredibly effective, can sometimes present challenges that may leave you scratching your head. One of the most common problems is inconsistent pressure maintenance. This often happens when the heat source fluctuates, causing the pressure inside the canner to rise and fall. Such inconsistencies can lead to under processed food, which is unsafe for long-term storage. Another issue is jar breakage during processing. This can occur if jars are not properly tempered or if they come into direct contact with the bottom of the canner. Food discoloration or texture changes are also frequent complaints.

These changes can result from improper processing times or temperatures, affecting both the safety and quality of the preserved food.

To address these issues, there are several practical solutions you can implement. First, ensure adequate water levels in the canner. Insufficient water can cause the canner to run dry, leading to fluctuating pressure and potential damage to the canner itself. Always check your canner's manual for the recommended water amount, usually around three quarts. Avoiding rapid temperature changes is another crucial step. Sudden changes can shock the jars, causing them to break. Gradually adjusting the heat and allowing the canner to cool naturally can prevent this. Adjusting processing times for altitude is also essential. Higher altitudes require longer processing times or increased pressure to compensate for the lower boiling point of water. Refer to altitude adjustment charts to ensure your food is processed safely.

Handling specific canning failures requires a good understanding of the signs and appropriate responses. If jars don't seal properly, don't panic. You can reprocess the jars within 24 hours. Simply replace the lid with a new one and reprocess for the full time specified in the recipe. Identifying signs of under processing is crucial. If you notice that the food inside the jars seems undercooked or if the jars did not reach the required pressure, it's best to reprocess them. Under processed food can be a breeding ground for bacteria, making it unsafe to eat. Safe disposal of spoiled food is another important aspect. If you suspect spoilage, such as off smells or visible mold, dispose of the food in a way that ensures it cannot be consumed by people or animals. Do not taste the food to check for spoilage, as even a small amount can cause severe illness.

Preventing these issues in future batches involves a combination of regular equipment maintenance and adhering to tested recipes and guidelines. Regularly check your canner's gauge for accuracy and inspect the gasket and other components for wear and tear. Keeping a detailed canning log can also be incredibly helpful. Record the types of food you've canned, the processing times and pressures used, and any issues encountered. This log can serve as a valuable reference for troubleshooting future batches and ensuring consistent results. By following these practices, you can significantly reduce the likelihood of encountering problems and enjoy the peace of mind that comes with safely preserved food.

A comprehensive understanding of the common problems and their solutions will make your pressure canning endeavors more successful and less stressful. Inconsistent pressure maintenance can be mitigated by monitoring the heat source closely and making gradual adjustments. Jar breakage can be prevented by ensuring jars are properly tempered and avoiding sudden changes in temperature. Addressing food discoloration and texture changes involves adhering to recommended processing times and temperatures. By handling specific canning failures with knowledge and care, you can recover from minor setbacks and continue preserving food safely. Regular maintenance and detailed logs are your best allies in achieving consistent, high-quality results.

3.5 ADVANCED PRESSURE CANNING TECHNIQUES

For those who have mastered the basics of pressure canning and are ready to explore more advanced techniques, there's a world of possibilities to elevate your preserving game. One exciting area to delve into is canning combination recipes like soups and stews. These recipes often combine various ingredients, including meats, vegetables, and broths, each with its own texture and flavor profile. When canning these complex dishes, it's essential to layer ingredients thoughtfully, ensuring even heat distribution. Using different jar sizes and types can also add versatility to your pantry. Quart jars are perfect for family-sized portions of beef stew, while pint jars are ideal for single-serving meals like chicken noodle soup.

Adjusting recipes for flavor and texture is another advanced technique that can significantly enhance your preserved foods. Adding herbs and spices to canned meats, for example, can transform a simple batch of chicken breasts into a gourmet delight. Think rosemary, thyme, or even a hint of smoked paprika. Creating flavorful broths and stocks is also a game-changer. These can be used as a base for soups or to add depth to various dishes. Don't shy away from preserving specialty items like seafood. Pressure canning shrimp or crab in a rich, seasoned broth can provide you with luxurious options that are ready to eat at a moment's notice.

Precision in measurements and timing is critical when tackling advanced canning projects. Measuring ingredients by weight ensures consistency, especially in recipes that require a delicate balance of flavors. For instance, weighing vegetables and meats before canning helps maintain the intended texture and taste. Accurately timing the processing is equally important. Use a reliable kitchen timer and start counting only when the canner reaches the correct pressure. Understanding the impact of ingredient variations is another key aspect. Slight changes, like using a different type of potato or varying the amount of salt, can affect the final product's safety and flavor.

Let's consider some advanced recipes to try.

Pressure Canned Beef Stew with Root Vegetables

A pressure-canned beef stew with root vegetables is a hearty meal perfect for cold winter nights. Start by browning beef chunks and then combine them with carrots, potatoes, and onions in a savory broth.

Chicken and Vegetable Soup with Herbs

For a lighter option, chicken and vegetable soup with herbs offers a comforting and nutritious meal. Use bone-in chicken pieces for richer flavor and add fresh herbs like parsley and dill for an aromatic touch.

Spicy Chili with Beans and Ground Beef

If you enjoy a bit of heat, spicy chili with beans and ground beef is an excellent choice. Add jalapenos, chili powder, and cumin to create a robust and spicy dish that can be enjoyed anytime.

Creating gourmet preserved foods involves a bit of creativity and experimentation. Don't be afraid to try new flavors and combinations. Adding a splash of white wine to a batch of canned mushrooms can elevate their taste, making them a delightful addition to sauces and sautés. Similarly, preserving peaches with a hint of vanilla and cinnamon can turn a simple fruit into a decadent dessert topping. The key is to maintain the balance of flavors while ensuring safe preservation practices.

Incorporating these advanced techniques into your pressure canning routine opens up a myriad of possibilities for delicious, ready-to-eat meals. Whether you're preparing for a busy week or stocking up for emergencies, these methods allow you to have a variety of flavorful and nutritious options at your fingertips. Precision, creativity, and a willingness to experiment are your best allies in this endeavor. By mastering these techniques, you'll not only enhance your culinary repertoire but also ensure that your pantry is always filled with high-quality, delightful foods.

Mastering advanced pressure canning techniques provides a deeper understanding of the process and offers the confidence to experiment with more complex recipes. As you become more comfortable with these methods, you'll find that the possibilities are endless. Up next, we'll explore the art of dehydrating foods, another versatile and valuable preservation method that complements your canning skills perfectly.

CHAPTER 4

DEHYDRATING FRUITS AND VEGETABLES

4.1 INTRODUCTION TO DEHYDRATING: BENEFITS AND BASICS

Dehydrating food is one of the oldest and simplest methods of preservation. The basic principle involves removing moisture from food to inhibit microbial growth. Microorganisms such as bacteria, yeasts, and molds require water to thrive. By removing this essential component, dehydration effectively extends the shelf life of food. The process typically involves low temperature drying, which helps retain the nutrients in the food. Unlike high-temperature methods, which can degrade vitamins and minerals, low-temperature drying preserves the food's nutritional value.

There are several methods to dehydrate food: sun drying, oven drying, and using an electric dehydrator.

Sun Drying

Sun drying is the oldest method, relying on the natural heat of the sun and good airflow to remove moisture. This method is cost-effective but weather-dependent and not ideal in humid climates.

Oven Drying

Oven drying is more accessible to most people, using the oven's low heat settings to dehydrate food. However, it can be energy-intensive and may not provide consistent results.

Electric Drying

An electric dehydrator is the most efficient and reliable method, offering precise temperature control and even drying. This device uses a fan and heating element to circulate warm air around the food, ensuring consistent dehydration.

Dehydrating food offers unique advantages over other preservation methods. One of the most notable benefits is the lightweight and compact storage. Dehydrated foods take up significantly less space than their fresh or canned counterparts, making them ideal for preppers who need to maximize storage capacity. The long shelf life of dehydrated foods, when stored properly, means you can enjoy seasonal produce year-round. Rehydration is straightforward and allows dehydrated foods to be used in a variety of dishes, from soups to stews. The process also retains the nutritional value and flavor of the food, making dehydrated snacks a healthier alternative to many store-bought options.

A wide range of foods can be successfully dehydrated. Fruits like apples, bananas, and berries are particularly well-suited for dehydration. These fruits retain their sweetness and make excellent snacks. Vegetables such as tomatoes, carrots, and peppers also dehydrate well. These can be rehydrated and added to soups, stews, and casseroles. Herbs and spices are another excellent option. Dehydrating these not only preserves their flavor but also concentrates it, making them a potent addition to your culinary repertoire.

Whether you choose to use an electric dehydrator, your oven, or the sun, the key is to remove moisture effectively while retaining the food's nutritional value and flavor. This method provides a versatile, space-saving solution for long-term food storage, making it an invaluable skill for anyone looking to become more self-sufficient.

4.2 CHOOSING THE RIGHT DEHYDRATOR FOR YOUR NEEDS

When it comes to dehydrating food, selecting the right dehydrator is crucial. There are several key features to consider ensuring you make an informed decision. Adjustable temperature settings are essential, allowing you to tailor the drying process to different types of food. For instance, fruits generally require a higher temperature than herbs. Fan and airflow design are also critical. A good dehydrator should have a fan that circulates air evenly, ensuring consistent drying across all trays. Tray capacity and expandability are important if you plan to dehydrate large quantities of food. Some models offer expandable trays, which can be a lifesaver during harvest season. Timer and auto shut-off features add convenience, allowing you to set it and forget it without worrying about over-drying your food.

Comparing different types and brands of dehydrators can help you find the best fit for your needs. Stackable dehydrators are generally more affordable and compact, making them a good choice for those with limited kitchen space. They are easy to store and can be expanded by adding more trays. However, they sometimes struggle with even airflow, especially in models where the fan is located at the bottom. On the other hand, shelf-style dehydrators are designed with trays that slide in and out like oven racks. This design offers superior airflow and more consistent drying but comes at a higher price point. High-end models like the Excalibur 6-Tray Dehydrator feature precise temperature and time control, ensuring optimal results every time. Budget-friendly options, such as the Nesco Snackmaster Pro Food Dehydrator, offer basic features and are perfect for beginners.

Each type of dehydrator has its pros and cons, which should be weighed based on your specific needs.

Stackable Dehydrator

Stackable dehydrators are affordable and compact, making them ideal for small kitchens or occasional use. They are easy to store and can be expanded by adding more trays. However, their limited airflow can result in uneven drying, requiring you to rotate trays occasionally.

Shelf-Style Dehydrator

Shelf-style dehydrators provide even drying and are more efficient, especially for large batches. They offer more precise temperature control and often come with additional features like timers and auto shut-off. However, they are bulkier and more expensive, making them a better choice for serious enthusiasts who plan to dehydrate frequently.

When it comes to recommendations based on user needs, it's important to consider how you plan to use your dehydrator. For beginners, simple models with basic features are often the best choice. The Nesco Snackmaster Pro Food Dehydrator is a great entry-level option. It offers stackable trays, adjustable temperature settings, and is easy to use. For those who plan to dehydrate large batches, high-capacity, shelf-style dehydrators like the Magic Mill Food Dehydrator are ideal. This model offers a larger drying area, consistent results, and features like a timer and auto shut-off. If you're focusing on herbs and delicate items, choose a model with precise temperature control. The COSORI Mini Food Dehydrator is compact, has presets for various foods, and is perfect for delicate herbs and spices.

Selecting the right dehydrator involves considering several factors, from adjustable temperature settings to tray capacity and airflow design. Whether you opt for a stackable or shelf-style model, the key is to find a dehydrator that meets your specific needs and fits your budget. With the right dehydrator, you'll be well-equipped to preserve a wide variety of foods, ensuring you can enjoy the bounty of your garden or market finds all year long.

4.3 PREPARING FRUITS AND VEGETABLES FOR DEHYDRATION

Before you can start dehydrating, it's crucial to properly prepare your fruits and vegetables. Begin by washing all produce thoroughly under cold running water. This step is essential to remove any dirt, pesticides, or bacteria. For some fruits and vegetables, peeling is necessary. Apples, for example, should be peeled to ensure a consistent texture, while tomatoes can be peeled to avoid tough skins in the final product. Once washed and peeled, slice the produce into uniform thickness. Aim for slices that are about 1/4 inch thick. This uniformity ensures even drying, as thinner pieces will dry faster than thicker ones, potentially leading to uneven results.

Certain vegetables benefit from blanching before dehydration. Blanching involves briefly boiling the vegetables and then plunging them into ice water to stop the cooking process. This step helps preserve the color, texture, and nutritional value of the vegetables. For instance, blanching carrots and green beans for a few minutes enhances their final texture and color. After blanching, make sure to pat the vegetables dry with a clean towel to remove excess moisture before placing them in the dehydrator.

Pre-treatment methods can significantly enhance the quality of your dehydrated products. One common method to prevent fruits like apples and bananas from browning is to dip them in a solution of lemon juice or ascorbic acid. This simple step helps maintain their appealing color and nutritional value. For fruits that you want to retain sweetness, consider syrup blanching. This involves boiling the fruit in a light sugar syrup before dehydrating. The syrup helps to keep the fruit moist and sweet. Vegetables can benefit from a salt or vinegar solution, which helps to preserve their color and flavor. Soaking sliced vegetables like bell peppers in a mild vinegar solution before dehydrating can enhance their taste and longevity.

When arranging produce on the dehydrator trays, proper spacing is key for optimal drying conditions. Avoid overlapping the slices as this can lead to uneven drying and potentially mold growth. Each piece should be placed in a single layer with enough space around it to allow air to circulate freely. For small items like herbs or berries, use mesh screens to prevent them from falling through the trays. Rotating the trays periodically during the drying process ensures even drying. Different areas of the dehydrator may have slightly different temperatures, so rotating the trays helps to equalize these variations.

Troubleshooting common preparation issues can save you a lot of frustration. Sticking and clumping are frequent problems, particularly with sugary fruits like mangoes. To prevent this, lightly spraying the trays with a non-stick spray before arranging the fruit can help. Uneven drying can often be corrected by adjusting the slice thickness. If some pieces are drying faster than others, it might be because they are thinner. Ensure all slices are of uniform thickness to avoid this issue. If you find that some slices are consistently drying unevenly, you might need to adjust the settings on your dehydrator or rotate the trays more frequently.

Proper washing, peeling, slicing, and pre-treating your produce ensures that the final product is of high quality and safe to consume. From preventing browning in fruits to enhancing the flavor of vegetables, each step plays a critical role in the dehydration process. Proper arrangement on the trays and regular monitoring can prevent common issues like sticking and uneven drying, ensuring that your dehydrated foods turn out perfectly every time.

4.4 STORING AND USING DEHYDRATED FOODS

Storing dehydrated foods properly ensures that they remain safe and delicious for a long time. The key to effective storage is keeping moisture out. Using airtight containers is essential. Mason jars, vacuum-sealed bags, and food-grade plastic containers work well. These containers prevent moisture from re-entering the food, which could lead to spoilage. Vacuum-sealed bags are particularly effective as they remove air, further reducing the risk of contamination. Another important aspect is to store your dehydrated foods in a cool, dark, and dry place. Heat, light, and humidity can degrade the quality and shelf life of dehydrated foods. A pantry or cupboard away from direct sunlight and heat sources is ideal. Regularly check your stored foods for signs of moisture or spoilage. If you notice any condensation inside the containers or a change in texture, it's best to use the food immediately or discard it.

The shelf life of dehydrated foods varies depending on the type of food and how well it is stored. Fruits generally have a long shelf life, lasting up to a year if stored properly. Their natural sugars act as preservatives, helping to maintain flavor and texture. Vegetables, depending on their type, can last between six to twelve months. Leafy greens and high-moisture vegetables like tomatoes may have a shorter shelf life compared to root vegetables like carrots and potatoes. Herbs and spices, when dehydrated, can retain their potency for up to two years. The key to maximizing shelf life is ensuring that the food is thoroughly dehydrated and stored in airtight conditions. Properly dried and stored foods not only last longer but also retain their nutritional value and flavor.

Using dehydrated foods in your meals is both practical and versatile. Rehydration is a simple process that allows you to incorporate dehydrated foods into a variety of dishes. Soaking dehydrated foods in water or broth before cooking can bring them back to life. For instance, rehydrated vegetables can be added to stir-fries, casseroles, or salads. Fruits can be soaked and used in baking or as toppings for cereals and yogurt. Dehydrated foods can also be used directly in soups and stews. They will absorb the liquid from the dish, rehydrating as they cook. This method is perfect for one-pot meals, making preparation quick and easy. Another creative way to use dehydrated foods is by grinding them into powders. Dehydrated tomatoes can be ground into a flavorful powder used in sauces, soups, and seasonings. Fruit powders can be added to smoothies, desserts, and baked goods for a burst of natural sweetness and color.

Managing your preserved food inventory can be challenging, especially if you have limited space. Creative storage solutions can help you maximize your storage capacity. Vacuum-sealed bags are an excellent choice for saving space. They can be stacked or tucked into small spaces, making them ideal for cramped pantries. Storing dehydrated foods in jars with desiccant packs can also extend their shelf life. Desiccant packs absorb any residual moisture, keeping your foods dry and fresh. Utilizing under-shelf storage and stackable containers can help you organize your pantry efficiently. Stackable containers make the most of vertical space, allowing you to store more in less space. Under-shelf baskets can provide additional storage without taking up valuable shelf space. These solutions not only help you manage your inventory but also keep your pantry organized and accessible.

By following these best practices for storing and using dehydrated foods, you can ensure long-term quality and safety. Proper storage techniques, such as using airtight containers and keeping foods in a cool, dark place, are crucial. Monitoring for signs of moisture or spoilage helps prevent waste and ensures that your preserved foods remain safe to eat.

Understanding the shelf life of various dehydrated foods allows you to plan and rotate your inventory effectively. Practical tips for rehydrating and using dehydrated foods make it easy to incorporate them into your meals, providing convenience and versatility. Creative storage solutions help you manage your preserved food inventory, making the most of your available space and keeping your pantry organized.

4.5 CREATIVE RECIPES WITH DEHYDRATED INGREDIENTS

When it comes to using dehydrated foods, the possibilities are nearly endless. Dehydrated ingredients can be the star of many innovative recipes. One classic example is trail mix. Combining dehydrated fruits like apples, bananas, and berries with nuts and seeds creates a nutritious and portable snack perfect for on-the-go energy. You can add a bit of dark chocolate or coconut flakes for extra flavor. Not only is this mix lightweight, but it also has a long shelf life, making it ideal for both preppers and everyday snackers.

Vegetable chips are another fantastic use for dehydrated produce. Slicing vegetables like sweet potatoes, zucchini, and beets thinly and dehydrating them results in crispy, healthy chips. These can be seasoned with a variety of spices—think garlic powder, paprika, or even a sprinkle of sea salt. They're a great alternative to store-bought chips and can be tailored to your taste preferences. Plus, they retain the nutritional benefits of the vegetables, offering a low-calorie, nutrient-dense snack option.

Homemade soup mixes are a convenient way to use dehydrated vegetables and herbs. Imagine a hearty vegetable soup mix that you can just add water or broth to and simmer for a quick meal. Combine dehydrated carrots, peas, corn, and potatoes with some dried herbs like parsley and thyme. Store these mixes in airtight jars, and you'll have a ready-to-go meal for busy days or emergencies. These mixes are easy to customize based on what you have available, making them versatile and practical.

Let's walk through some step-by-step instructions for these recipes.

Trail Mix

For trail mix, gather 1 cup of dehydrated apple slices, 1 cup of dehydrated banana chips, 1/2 cup of dried berries, 1 cup of mixed nuts, and 1/4 cup of dark chocolate chunks. Mix all the ingredients in a large bowl and store in an airtight container.

Vegetable Chips

For vegetable chips, slice your vegetables to about 1/8 inch thick. Arrange them in a single layer on your dehydrator trays, sprinkle with your choice of seasoning, and dehydrate at 125°F for 6-8 hours until crisp.

Soup Mix

For the soup mix, combine 1 cup of dehydrated carrots, 1 cup of dehydrated peas, 1 cup of dehydrated corn, 1 cup of dehydrated potatoes, and 1 tablespoon of dried parsley. Mix well and store in a jar.

Dehydrated foods are packed with nutritional benefits that make them a valuable addition to your diet. Dehydrated fruits retain their high fiber content, which aids digestion and keeps you feeling full longer. The low-temperature drying process helps retain vitamins and minerals in vegetables, ensuring you get the nutritional benefits without the loss that can occur with other preservation methods. Moreover, dehydrated foods are low in calories, making them a smart choice for healthy snacking. Whether you're munching on vegetable chips or adding dried fruits to your breakfast, you're getting a nutrient-dense snack that's both satisfying and beneficial.

Incorporating dehydrated foods into everyday meals can be both practical and creative. Adding dehydrated vegetables to pasta sauces and casseroles is a simple way to boost the nutritional content of your meals. Just toss the dried veggies into the sauce as it simmers, and they'll rehydrate while cooking, blending seamlessly into the dish. Fruit powders made from dehydrated fruits can be a game-changer in smoothies and baked goods. Add a spoonful of apple or strawberry powder to your morning smoothie for a burst of flavor and nutrients. Dehydrated herbs and spices can be ground into fine powders to create custom seasoning blends. Imagine a homemade Italian seasoning mix with dehydrated basil, oregano, and thyme, ready to sprinkle on your favorite dishes.

The versatility of dehydrated foods makes them an invaluable resource in the kitchen. They offer convenience, long shelf life, and nutritional benefits that are hard to match. Whether you're preparing snacks, quick meals, or enhancing the flavors of your everyday dishes, dehydrated ingredients can elevate your culinary creations. By exploring the various ways to use dehydrated foods, you'll not only make the most of your preserved harvest but also enjoy a diverse and nutritious diet. This chapter has shown just a few of the creative possibilities, leading us seamlessly into the next topic—fermenting for flavor and health.

CHAPTER 5

FERMENTING FOR FLAVOR AND HEALTH

5.1 THE SCIENCE OF FERMENTATION: HOW IT WORKS

Fermentation is a fascinating process where beneficial bacteria transform food, enhancing both its flavor and nutritional value. At its core, fermentation involves lactic acid bacteria (LAB) converting sugars into lactic acid. This conversion is what gives fermented foods their characteristic tangy flavor. Lactobacillus, a type of LAB found naturally on plants and in dairy, plays a pivotal role in this process. When given the right conditions—absence of oxygen and the presence of sugars—these bacteria thrive. As they consume sugars, they produce lactic acid, which lowers the pH of the food, creating an environment that inhibits harmful bacteria and preserves the food.

Creating an anaerobic (oxygen-free) environment is crucial in fermentation. This environment allows beneficial bacteria to flourish while keeping unwanted microbes at bay. When you submerge vegetables in a brine solution, you effectively seal them off from oxygen. This is why using weights to keep the produce submerged is so important. The lack of oxygen coupled with the production of lactic acid creates a hostile environment for spoilage organisms and pathogens. The result is a safe, preserved food product that can last for months.

The health benefits of fermented foods are extensive. Fermentation increases the bioavailability of nutrients, meaning your body can absorb them more efficiently. For example, the fermentation process can increase the levels of certain vitamins in foods. Sauerkraut, for instance, is higher in vitamin C than raw cabbage. The probiotics produced during fermentation are another significant benefit. These beneficial bacteria promote gut health by balancing the gut microbiome, aiding digestion, and enhancing immune support. Regular consumption of fermented foods can improve digestive health, reducing symptoms like bloating and constipation. Moreover, a healthy gut microbiome has been linked to improved mood and reduced anxiety.

Different types of fermentation serve various purposes and applications. Lactic acid fermentation is perhaps the most common, used for vegetables like sauerkraut and kimchi, as well as dairy products like yogurt. This method relies on LAB to convert sugars into lactic acid, preserving the food and enhancing its flavor. Alcohol fermentation is another type, used for beverages such as kombucha and kefir. In this process, yeast converts sugars into alcohol and carbon dioxide. Kombucha, for example, undergoes a two-step fermentation process, first by yeast and then by bacteria, resulting in a fizzy, tangy drink. Acetic acid fermentation is used to produce vinegar. In this method, bacteria convert alcohol into acetic acid, which gives vinegar its sour taste and preservative qualities.

Salt plays a crucial role in the fermentation process. It creates an environment that favors the growth of beneficial bacteria while inhibiting the growth of spoilage organisms. Adding the right amount of salt ensures that the fermentation process proceeds smoothly. For most vegetables, a salt concentration of around 2% of the weight of the vegetables is ideal. This concentration is enough to draw out water from the vegetables, creating a brine that submerges them and keeps them anaerobic. Salt also helps to maintain the crisp texture of fermented vegetables by inhibiting the enzymes that cause vegetables to soften.

By mastering the science behind fermentation, you can unlock its full potential, turning basic ingredients into nutritious and flavorful foods. The fundamental principles apply whether you're fermenting beverages, dairy, or vegetables. Creating the ideal environment for beneficial bacteria allows you to produce an array of preserved, delicious foods that offer substantial health advantages.

The next time you savor a tangy bite of sauerkraut or sip on a refreshing glass of kombucha, you can admire the extraordinary process that brought them to life.

5.2 ESSENTIAL FERMENTATION EQUIPMENT AND SUPPLIES

When you venture into the world of fermentation, having the right equipment can make all the difference. To start, you'll need fermentation crocks and jars. These vessels are where the magic happens. Fermentation crocks are traditional and durable, often made from ceramic. They are perfect for large batches of sauerkraut or kimchi. Glass jars, on the other hand, are more affordable and widely available. You can find them in various sizes, making them versatile for different types of ferments. For beginners, wide-mouth glass jars are particularly handy as they make packing and cleaning easier.

Weights and airlocks are crucial for maintaining an anaerobic environment, which is essential for successful fermentation. Weights keep the vegetables submerged in the brine, preventing exposure to air and potential mold growth. You can find weights made from glass or ceramic, both of which are effective. Airlocks allow gases produced during fermentation to escape without letting air in. This helps in preventing the buildup of pressure and keeps the environment anaerobic. Fermentation lids and seals are also important. These specially designed lids fit onto your jars and often come with built-in airlocks, making the process more straightforward. Lids with silicone gaskets provide a tight seal, further ensuring no unwanted air gets in.

Choosing the right fermentation vessel depends on your needs and preferences. Glass jars are a popular choice due to their affordability and availability. They are transparent, allowing you to see the fermentation process, and they don't retain odors or stains. However, they are fragile and can break if handled roughly. Ceramic crocks are another excellent option. They are traditional, durable, and maintain a consistent temperature, which is beneficial for fermentation. The downside is that they can be heavy and more expensive. Plastic containers are lightweight and less likely to break, but they may leach chemicals into your ferment, especially if they are not food-grade. It's best to avoid plastic unless it's specifically labeled as safe for fermentation.

Using non-reactive materials is crucial for safety in fermentation. Metal containers should be avoided as they can react with the acids produced during fermentation, potentially leaching harmful substances into your food. Food-grade plastic and glass are the safest options. Glass is non-reactive and doesn't absorb flavors or odors, making it ideal for repeated use. Food-grade plastic can be used but ensure it's BPA-free and specifically designed for food storage. Ceramic is another non-reactive option, perfect for larger batches and long-term use. Always check that your materials are food-safe to avoid contamination.

Sourcing and maintaining your fermentation equipment requires some attention to detail. Cleaning and sterilizing vessels before use is the first step. Use hot, soapy water to clean your jars and crocks, and rinse them thoroughly. For an extra layer of safety, you can sterilize them by boiling or using a dishwasher with a sterilize setting. Inspecting seals and airlocks for proper function is essential. Make sure there are no cracks or damages that could compromise the anaerobic environment. Purchasing supplies from reputable sources ensures you get quality equipment. Look for brands known for their durability and safety standards. Online reviews can also guide you in making informed choices.

Taking good care of your fermentation equipment ensures longevity and successful ferments. Regular cleaning prevents the buildup of residues that could harbor harmful bacteria. After each use, clean your jars, lids, and weights thoroughly. Store them in a dry place to avoid mold and mildew. If you notice any damage or wear, replace the parts as needed. Investing in good-quality equipment and maintaining it properly will make your fermentation endeavors smoother and more enjoyable, allowing you to focus on creating delicious, healthy ferments.

5.3 FERMENTING VEGETABLES: STEP-BY-STEP GUIDE

Fermenting vegetables begins with selecting and preparing your produce. Choose fresh, high-quality vegetables for the best results. Organic options are ideal, as they are free from pesticides that could interfere with fermentation. Start by washing your vegetables thoroughly under cold running water. This step removes dirt and bacteria that could spoil the ferment. Depending on the vegetable, you may need to peel it. For example, carrots and radishes often benefit from peeling, while cucumbers can be left with their skins on if they are thin and tender. Once washed and peeled, slice or chop your vegetables into even pieces. Uniformity ensures they ferment at the same rate.

Creating a brine solution is the next crucial step. The brine is simply a mixture of water and salt, which helps create the ideal environment for fermentation. For most vegetables, a 2% salt solution works well. This means you'll need about 20 grams of salt per liter of water. Use non-iodized salt, such as sea salt or himalayan pink salt, as iodine can inhibit fermentation. Dissolve the salt in water, ensuring it is completely mixed. If you prefer a more precise approach, you can weigh the vegetables and water to get the exact ratio. Pour the brine over the vegetables, ensuring they are fully submerged. Keeping the vegetables submerged is essential to create an anaerobic environment, which promotes the growth of beneficial bacteria while inhibiting harmful ones.

Packing the vegetables into fermentation vessels is a methodical process. Use clean, sterilized jars or crocks for this purpose. Begin by adding a layer of vegetables to the bottom of the vessel. Press down firmly with a tamper or a clean hand to pack them tightly and remove air pockets. Continue adding layers and pressing until the vessel is nearly full, leaving about an inch of headspace at the top. This space allows for the expansion of gases produced during fermentation. Pour the brine over the packed vegetables, ensuring they are completely submerged. Placing a weight on top of the vegetables helps keep them below the brine. This weight can be a specialized fermentation weight or a clean, heavy object like a small plate or a jar filled with water.

Ensuring successful fermentation involves a few key practices. Maintaining a consistent temperature is one of the most important factors. Most vegetables ferment best at temperatures between 65°F and 75°F. Too warm, and the fermentation process can proceed too quickly, leading to off-flavors and mushy textures. Too cold, and it can slow down or stop altogether. Place your fermentation vessel in a cool, dark place, such as a pantry or cupboard, to maintain a stable temperature. Regularly check for air bubbles and scum formation on the surface. Air bubbles are a normal part of the fermentation process, but scum should be removed promptly to prevent spoilage.

Fermentation timeframes vary depending on the type of vegetable. Cabbage, for example, can take anywhere from one to four weeks to ferment fully. The length of time depends on the fermentation temperature and your taste preference. Carrots and radishes typically ferment more quickly, usually within one to two weeks. They are ready when they have a tangy flavor and a slightly softened texture. Cucumbers also ferment within one to two weeks. They should retain a bit of crunch while developing a pleasantly sour taste. Taste your ferments periodically to determine when they are ready. Once they reach the desired flavor and texture, transfer them to the refrigerator to slow down the fermentation process and preserve them for longer periods.

A successful fermentation experience comes from following these essential steps and tips. The process begins with selecting and preparing the appropriate vegetables, followed by making an effective brine solution and carefully packing everything into fermentation vessels. Regularly monitoring the process and maintaining the proper conditions help you avoid common issues and ensure the vegetables ferment as they should. With practice and patience, you'll soon be creating tangy, delicious, fermented vegetables that not only taste amazing but also provide various health benefits.

5.4 MAKING YOUR OWN SAUERKRAUT AND KIMCHI

Making sauerkraut at home is a rewarding and straightforward process that starts with selecting the right cabbage. Choose fresh, firm heads of cabbage, preferably organic. Begin by removing the outer leaves and cutting the cabbage into quarters. Shred the cabbage finely using a sharp knife or a mandoline slicer. The thinner the shreds, the more surface area for the salt to work on, which speeds up the fermentation process. Place the shredded cabbage in a large mixing bowl, sprinkle it with salt, and let it sit for a few minutes. The salt will draw out the natural juices from the cabbage, creating the brine needed for fermentation.

Next, massage the cabbage with your hands, squeezing it firmly. This action helps release more juice and breaks down the cell walls of the cabbage, making it more pliable. Continue massaging until the cabbage becomes limp and you see a good amount of liquid at the bottom of the bowl. This process usually takes about 5-10 minutes. Once the cabbage is sufficiently massaged, it's time to pack it into jars. Use a clean, wide-mouth jar and pack the cabbage tightly, pressing it down firmly with a tamper or the back of a spoon. Ensure the cabbage is submerged in its own juices to create an anaerobic environment, vital for successful fermentation.

Adding variations and flavor to your sauerkraut can make each batch unique. One popular addition is caraway seeds, which add a savory, slightly nutty flavor. You can also try juniper berries for a slightly piney, aromatic twist. For a colorful and nutrient-packed kraut, mix in shredded carrots or beets. These vegetables not only add vibrant color but also extra nutrients and a slight sweetness. Experiment with different types of cabbage, like red or Napa, to see how they change the flavor and texture. Each variation brings its own unique taste and benefits, making your sauerkraut both delicious and nutritious.

Making traditional kimchi involves a few more steps but is equally rewarding. Start with Napa cabbage, which is the backbone of kimchi. Cut the cabbage lengthwise into quarters, then cut each quarter into bite-sized pieces. Soak the cabbage in a saltwater solution for a couple of hours to soften it. While the cabbage is soaking, prepare the other ingredients. Peel and julienne daikon radish, chop green onions, and mince garlic and ginger. For the spicy paste, mix Korean chili flakes (gochugaru) with fish sauce, sugar, and a bit of water to create a thick, red paste. Adjust the amount of chili flakes to your taste preference.

Once the cabbage has softened, rinse it thoroughly to remove excess salt and drain well. Mix the cabbage with the prepared vegetables and spicy paste, ensuring everything is evenly coated. Pack the mixture tightly into a fermentation jar or crock, pressing down firmly to remove air pockets. Leave some headspace at the top, as the kimchi will expand as it ferments. Place a weight on top to keep the vegetables submerged in the brine. Seal the jar with a lid, making sure it's airtight. Let the kimchi ferment at room temperature for a few days to a week, depending on the ambient temperature and your taste preference. The longer it ferments, the tangier and more complex the flavor will become.

Sauerkraut and kimchi are not only flavorful but also packed with health benefits. Both are rich in vitamins C and K, essential for immune function and bone health. The fermentation process increases the bioavailability of these vitamins, making them easier for your body to absorb. Additionally, sauerkraut and kimchi are teeming with lactobacilli and other beneficial bacteria. These probiotics support a healthy gut microbiome, aiding digestion and boosting overall immune health. The anti-inflammatory proper-ties of fermented foods can also help reduce digestive discomfort and improve nutrient absorption. Including sauerkraut and kimchi in your diet can provide a delicious way to enhance your health and wellbeing, making them valuable additions to any meal.

5.5 TROUBLESHOOTING FERMENTATION: COMMON PROBLEMS AND SOLUTIONS

Fermentation can sometimes present challenges, but under-standing common issues can help you navigate them with confi-dence. One of the most frequent problems is mold growth on the surface of your ferment. Mold can appear as white, blue, green, or black spots and usually forms when vegetables are exposed to air. This exposure can happen if the vegetables are not fully submerged in the brine. Another issue is unpleasant odors or flavors, which can result from improper fermentation conditions. These off-smells may be due to contamination or an imbalance in the microbial population. Vegetables becoming too soft or mushy is another common problem. This often occurs when the fermentation process is too fast, or the salt concentration is too low.

Addressing these issues involves several practical steps. If you notice mold growth, carefully remove the moldy layer using a clean spoon. Ensure the remaining vegetables are still submerged in the brine. Adjusting brine levels can also help; add more brine if necessary to keep everything submerged. Proper ventilation and airlock function are crucial to prevent mold and ensure a healthy ferment. Make sure your airlock is functioning correctly and releasing gases without letting air in. Adjusting salt concentration and fermentation time can also resolve many issues. A higher salt concentration can slow down the fermentation, preventing vegetables from becoming too soft. Similarly, monitoring and adjusting fermentation time based on temperature and taste can help achieve the desired texture and flavor.

Knowing how to handle specific fermentation failures can save your batch and build your confidence. Identifying signs of spoilage is the first step. Spoiled ferments often have a foul odor, slimy texture, or visible mold that cannot be easily removed. If you suspect spoilage, it's best to err on the side of caution. Safe disposal of spoiled batches is essential; discard the batch in a way that prevents cross-contamination with other ferments or foods. This might involve sealing it in a plastic bag and disposing of it in the trash. Preventing cross-contamination in future batches involves thorough cleaning and sterilizing of all equipment and surfaces. Ensure that your hands and tools are clean before handling any new batches.

Preventing issues in future batches starts with regular monitoring of your fermentation vessels. Check your ferments daily for the first week and then every few days afterward. Look for any signs of mold, off-smells, or changes in brine levels. Maintaining a clean and sterile environment is also crucial. Clean your workspace and equipment thoroughly before starting a new batch. Using food-grade cleaning solutions can help ensure that no harmful residues are left behind. Keeping detailed fermentation logs can be incredibly helpful. Record the type of vegetables, salt concentration, fermentation temperature, and any issues encountered. This log can serve as a valuable reference for troubleshooting and improving future batches.

By understanding these common issues and their solutions, you can ensure consistent and successful fermentation results. Regular monitoring, maintaining cleanliness, and keeping detailed records are all practices that contribute to a smooth fermentation process. With these tips, you can confidently tackle any challenges that arise and enjoy the many benefits of homemade fermented foods.

In this chapter, we've explored the science behind fermentation, essential equipment, and detailed steps for fermenting vegetables and making sauerkraut and kimchi. We've also covered practical solutions to common fermentation issues. These insights and techniques equip you with the knowledge to preserve food in a way that enhances its flavor and nutritional value. Next, we'll delve into freezing, another versatile method for long-term food storage.

YOUR FEEDBACK IS VALUED!

Thank you for purchasing *The Preserver's Handbook: Your Essential Guide to Canning, Preserving, Fermenting, Freezing, and Dehydrating for Long-Term Storage.* I hope this book has been an invaluable resource on your journey to mastering the art of food preservation. Your feedback is essential in helping others discover the benefits of preserving their own food.

If you found this book helpful, I'd be so grateful if you could take a moment to leave a **5-star** review on Amazon.

★★★★★

It costs nothing, but your review can make a world of difference in helping others, just like you, find this book. Every review not only supports my work but also increases the chances that this message will reach more people. Your thoughts on what helped you, what you liked most, or even areas where you'd like more information in future volumes, will help us create even better resources for gardeners like you.

HOW TO LEAVE A REVIEW:

1. Visit the book's page on Amazon.
2. Scroll down to the "Customer Reviews" section.
3. Click "Write a customer review" and share your thoughts!

Happy gardening!

—The Grinning Gardener

CHAPTER 6
FREEZING FOR LONG-TERM STORAGE

6.1 INTRODUCTION TO FREEZING: BENEFITS AND DRAWBACKS

Freezing is a straightforward yet powerful method for preserving food. At its core, freezing works by slowing down enzyme activity and microbial growth. Enzymes are proteins that speed up chemical reactions, such as ripening and spoilage in fruits and vegetables. When you freeze food, the low temperatures slow these enzymes down, effectively pausing the ripening process and preserving the food's quality. Similarly, freezing halts the activity of microorganisms, such as bacteria and molds, that cause food to spoil. By keeping food at 0°F (-18°C) or lower, you can extend its shelf life significantly while maintaining its nutritional value and flavor.

One of the biggest advantages of freezing is its convenience and ease of use. Unlike canning or dehydrating, which require specific equipment and precise techniques, freezing is relatively simple. You can freeze a wide range of foods with minimal preparation. Additionally, freezing results in minimal nutrient loss compared to other methods. Vitamins and minerals are well-preserved, making frozen foods a healthy option for long-term storage. The versatility of freezing is another major benefit. You can preserve fruits, vegetables, meats, seafood, dairy products, and even baked goods. This flexibility allows you to make the most of seasonal produce and bulk purchases.

However, freezing does have its drawbacks. Freezer burn is a common issue that occurs when food is exposed to air, causing it to dry out and develop off-flavors. This can be mitigated by using airtight containers or vacuum sealing. Texture changes are another potential downside. Ice crystals that form during freezing can break down the cell walls of fruits and vegetables, resulting in a mushy texture when thawed. Energy costs are also a consideration. Running a freezer continuously requires electricity, which can add to your utility bills. Additionally, space limitations can be a challenge, especially if you are freezing large quantities of food. A well-organized freezer can help maximize storage capacity, but it's important to plan accordingly.

When it comes to what to freeze, the possibilities are extensive. Fruits like berries, apples, and peaches freeze exceptionally well. Vegetables such as green beans, carrots, and broccoli also retain their quality when frozen, especially if blanched beforehand. Meats and seafood are excellent candidates for freezing, maintaining their texture and flavor for months. Dairy products, including cheese, butter, and milk, can be frozen, although some may experience slight texture changes. Baked goods like bread, muffins, and cookies also freeze beautifully, making it easy to enjoy homemade treats whenever you like.

However, not all foods are suitable for freezing. High-water content items, such as lettuce, cucumber, and watermelon, do not freeze well. The water inside these foods expands when frozen, breaking down the cell structure and resulting in a mushy texture when thawed. Similarly, mayonnaise-based dishes and cream sauces can separate and become unappetizing after freezing. It's best to avoid freezing these types of foods and instead focus on items that retain their quality and texture.

Freezing offers a convenient and versatile solution for preserving a wide range of foods while maintaining their nutritional value. By understanding the benefits and potential drawbacks, you can make informed decisions about what to freeze and how to do it effectively. Whether you're looking to preserve a seasonal bounty or stock up for emergencies, freezing is a valuable tool in your food preservation arsenal.

6.2 PREPARING FOODS FOR FREEZING: BLANCHING AND PACKAGING

Preparing your produce properly before freezing is key to maintaining its quality and flavor. Start with washing and trimming your fruits and vegetables. Use cold running water to remove dirt and pesticides. For vegetables, trim away any damaged or inedible parts. Fruits like apples and pears should be peeled and cored, while berries can be left whole. Slicing and dicing is the next step. Uniform pieces ensure even freezing and thawing. For example, slice carrots into coins and chop bell peppers into strips. This makes it easier to use them straight from the freezer without additional prep.

Blanching vegetables is an important step to preserve their color, texture, and nutritional value. Blanching involves briefly boiling vegetables to inactivate enzymes that can cause spoilage and then quickly cooling them in ice water. This process also destroys microorganisms on the surface of the vegetables. To blanch, fill a large pot with water and bring it to a vigorous boil. Use one gallon of water per pound of vegetables. Place the vegetables in a blanching basket and lower them into the boiling water, covering the pot with a lid. The water should return to a boil within a minute. If it doesn't, you've added too many vegetables. Start counting your blanching time once the water returns to a boil. For instance, green beans need about three minutes, while broccoli should blanch for about three minutes as well. After blanching, transfer the vegetables immediately to a bowl of ice water to stop the cooking process. Once cooled, drain and dry the vegetables thoroughly before freezing.

Proper packaging is crucial to prevent freezer burn and maintain the quality of your frozen foods. Freezer burn occurs when food is exposed to air, causing it to dry out and develop off-flavors. To avoid this, use airtight containers or freezer bags. Remove as much air as possible before sealing. Vacuum sealers are particularly effective, but if you don't have one, you can use a straw to suck out air from a zip-top bag. Double-wrapping foods provides extra protection. For example, wrap meats in freezer paper before placing them in a freezer bag. This extra layer helps preserve flavor and texture.

Labeling and dating your frozen foods is essential for keeping track of what you have and ensuring you use items before they lose quality. Use waterproof markers and labels to clearly mark each package with the contents and the date of freezing. For example, write "Blanched Carrots - 10/20/23" on the bag. This helps you quickly identify what's inside and when it was frozen. Rotating stock is another important practice. Place newer items at the back and older ones at the front. This ensures you use the oldest items first, reducing waste and maintaining a steady supply of fresh ingredients.

Freezing is a versatile method that, with proper preparation, can preserve a wide range of foods. By washing, trimming, slicing, and blanching your produce, you set the stage for successful long-term storage. Proper packaging, labeling, and dating further ensure that your frozen foods remain in top condition. Each of these steps plays a crucial role in maintaining the quality, flavor, and nutritional value of your frozen produce, making it a reliable option for preserving your harvest and reducing food waste.

6.3 BEST PRACTICES FOR FREEZING FRUITS AND VEGETABLES

Freezing fruits and vegetables can be a game-changer when it comes to preserving the bounty of your garden or bulk purchases. For fruits, it's crucial to tailor your approach based on the type. Berries, for instance, should be frozen individually before packaging. Spread them out on a baking sheet in a single layer and place them in the freezer. Once they are completely frozen, transfer them to a freezer bag. This method prevents the berries from clumping together, allowing you to grab a handful at a time. Delicate fruits like peaches benefit from using sugar packs or syrup packs. Slice the peaches and mix them with sugar or syrup before freezing. This not only preserves their texture but also enhances their sweetness. Apples and pears, which tend to brown quickly, should be treated with lemon juice. After slicing, toss them in a mixture of one tablespoon lemon juice per cup of water. This simple step keeps them looking fresh and appetizing.

When it comes to vegetables, blanching is your best friend. This process inactivates enzymes that can cause spoilage and helps maintain color and texture. Blanching times vary depending on the vegetable. For example, broccoli and green beans need about three minutes, while carrots sliced into coins should be blanched for around five minutes. Leafy greens like spinach and kale should be blanched and then packed in small portions. This makes it easier to use just what you need without having to thaw a large amount. Delicate vegetables like asparagus benefit from steam blanching. Instead of boiling, use a steamer basket to gently blanch the asparagus for about two to four minutes, depending on the thickness of the stalks. This method retains their crisp texture and vibrant color.

Maintaining texture and flavor in frozen produce requires a few additional steps. Flash freezing is highly effective. After blanching and cooling your vegetables, spread them out on a baking sheet in a single layer and freeze them. Once frozen, transfer them to airtight containers or freezer bags. This technique helps maintain the individual pieces and makes it easier to use just what you need. Using vacuum sealers to remove air from the packaging can prevent freezer burn and preserve flavor. If you don't have a vacuum sealer, a simple straw can help remove excess air from zip-top bags.

Common freezing issues like freezer burn and texture changes can be frustrating. Freezer burn occurs when food is exposed to air, leading to dry, tough patches. Prevent this by using proper packaging techniques. Always use airtight containers or freezer bags and remove as much air as possible before sealing. Labeling your packages with the date can help you keep track of how long items have been in the freezer, reducing the risk of freezer burn. Texture changes, especially in fruits and vegetables, are often due to ice crystal formation. Large ice crystals can break down cell walls, leading to mushy produce when thawed. Flash freezing and vacuum sealing can help minimize this issue. If you notice that your frozen fruits and vegetables have developed ice crystals, it's best to use them in cooked dishes where texture is less of a concern.

By following these best practices, you can freeze a wide variety of fruits and vegetables while maintaining their quality and flavor. Tailoring your approach to each type of produce, blanching vegetables correctly, and using proper packaging techniques can make a significant difference. Whether you're preparing for the winter months or simply making the most of seasonal abundance, freezing can be a reliable and effective method for long-term food storage.

6.4 FREEZING MEATS AND SEAFOOD: STEP-BY-STEP

Freezing meats is a straightforward process that ensures your proteins are ready to go when you need them. Start by trimming any excess fat from the meat. Fat doesn't freeze well and can become rancid, affecting the overall quality. Once trimmed, portion the meat into sizes that suit your needs. For example, cut chicken breasts into single-serving sizes or divide ground meat into one-pound portions. This step makes it easier to thaw exactly what you need without wasting any food.

After portioning, wrap the meat in freezer paper. This helps protect it from freezer burn by creating a barrier between the meat and the cold air. Once wrapped, place the meat in a vacuum-sealed bag or a high-quality freezer bag. Removing as much air as possible is crucial to preserving the meat's texture and flavor. Label each package with the type of meat and the date of freezing. This helps you keep track of what you have and ensures you use the oldest items first.

Freezing seafood requires a slightly different approach but follows the same basic principles. Start by cleaning and deboning the fish. Fillets should be rinsed under cold water and patted dry with paper towels. For shellfish like shrimp and scallops, it's best to flash freeze them individually. Lay them out on a baking sheet in a single layer and freeze until solid. Once frozen, transfer them to a freezer bag. This prevents them from sticking together and allows you to take out only what you need. Another excellent technique for seafood is ice glazing. Dip the seafood in ice water and place it on a baking sheet. Once a thin layer of ice forms, repeat the process until you have a protective glaze. This extra layer helps maintain moisture and flavor.

Proper thawing methods are essential for maintaining the quality and safety of your frozen meats and seafood. The safest way to thaw is in the refrigerator. This method ensures an even defrosting process and keeps the meat at a safe temperature. Place the frozen meat or seafood in a dish to catch any drips and allow it to thaw for several hours or overnight. If you need to thaw quickly, use a cold-water bath. Place the sealed package in a bowl of cold water, changing the water every 30 minutes to keep it cold.

Avoid thawing at room temperature, as this can lead to bacterial growth and foodborne illnesses.

To maintain the quality and flavor of your frozen meats, consider freezing them in marinades. This not only adds flavor but also helps keep the meat tender. For example, marinate chicken breasts in a mixture of olive oil, lemon juice, and herbs before freezing. When you're ready to cook, the meat will already be infused with delicious flavors. Using butcher's wrap followed by freezer bags provides an extra layer of protection against freezer burn. This double wrapping method is especially useful for meats that you plan to store for several months. Always rotate your stock to ensure that older items are used first, maintaining a fresh supply.

By following these steps, you can ensure that your meats and seafood remain high-quality and flavorful for months. Proper trimming, portioning, and packaging are key to preventing freezer burn and maintaining texture. Safe thawing methods and thoughtful practices like marinating add convenience and enhance the taste of your frozen foods. Whether you're stocking up on proteins for everyday meals or preparing for emergencies, these techniques will help you make the most of your freezer space and keep your food supply fresh and delicious.

6.5 MAXIMIZING FREEZER SPACE: ORGANIZATION AND STORAGE TIPS

When you're dealing with limited freezer space, efficient organization becomes critical. One effective strategy is to use bins and baskets to categorize items. By grouping similar foods together, you can easily find what you need without rummaging through the entire freezer. For example, designate one bin for vegetables, another for meats, and yet another for fruits. Labeling shelves and sections further enhance accessibility. Use clear, easy-to-read labels to identify each section, making it simple for everyone in the household to know where items belong. Implementing a first-in, first-out (FIFO) system ensures that you use older items first, reducing waste and keeping your stock fresh.

Optimizing freezer space also involves practical storage techniques. Using vacuum-sealed bags is a great way to reduce bulk. These bags compress the food, removing excess air and making it easier to stack items neatly. Stacking flat packages is another space-saving method. Instead of bulky containers, freeze items in flat, stackable packages. This not only saves space but also makes it easier to organize your freezer. For liquids, consider freezing them in ice cube trays before transferring them to bags. This method is particularly useful for broths, sauces, and even herbs in olive oil. Once frozen, pop the cubes into a bag and store them neatly without taking up too much space.

Maintaining an organized freezer requires regular upkeep. Start by setting a schedule for cleaning and defrosting your freezer. This helps prevent ice buildup, which can reduce storage space and efficiency. Conduct periodic inventory checks to know what you have and what needs to be used soon. Keeping a freezer log is another effective practice. Record the contents, date of freezing, and any notes about the items. This log can be a simple notebook or a digital spreadsheet, whatever works best for you. Regularly updating this log ensures you always know what's in your freezer and can plan meals accordingly.

For those with limited freezer space, creativity in storage solutions is key. Prioritize high-value items for freezing, such as meats and vegetables, which benefit most from long-term storage. Using chest freezers can provide additional storage capacity. These freezers are often more energy-efficient and can hold larger quantities of food. If space is still an issue, consider sharing freezer space with neighbors or family members. This can be particularly useful for bulk purchases or when preserving a large harvest. Coordinating with others can maximize the use of available space and ensure that everyone benefits from the efficiency of bulk storage.

In summary, efficient freezer organization and smart storage techniques can make a significant difference in how much you can store and how easy it is to access your frozen goods. By using bins and baskets, labeling sections, and implementing a FIFO system, you can keep your freezer organized and reduce food waste. Practical storage tips like vacuum-sealing, stacking flat packages, and freezing liquids in ice cube trays help maximize space. Regular maintenance, inventory checks, and keeping a freezer log ensure long-term organization and efficiency. For those with limited space, prioritizing high-value items, utilizing chest freezers, and sharing storage can provide practical solutions.

These strategies not only make the most of your freezer space but also ensure that your preserved foods remain in optimal condition. Proper organization and storage are crucial for maintaining the quality and longevity of your frozen goods. As you implement these tips, you'll find that managing your freezer becomes a more streamlined and efficient process. With a well-organized freezer, you can easily access your preserved foods, reduce waste, and enjoy the benefits of long-term storage. Now, let's explore the fascinating world of advanced preservation techniques in the next chapter.

CHAPTER 7
ADVANCED PRESERVATION TECHNIQUES

7.1 FREEZE-DRYING AT HOME: EQUIPMENT AND TECHNIQUES

F reeze-drying, also known as lyophilization, is an advanced dehydration process that removes moisture from food while preserving its structure, nutrients, and flavor. The science behind freeze-drying involves three main stages: freezing, sublimation, and desorption. Initially, food is frozen under atmospheric pressure, turning its water content into ice. This step is crucial as it sets the stage for the sublimation process. During sublimation, the frozen water is removed directly as vapor without passing through the liquid phase. This is achieved by lowering the pressure in a vacuum chamber, allowing the ice to transition directly into gas. Finally, the desorption stage removes any remaining bound water molecules, ensuring the food is thoroughly dried. This meticulous process maintains the food's cellular structure, resulting in lightweight, shelf-stable products that retain their original texture and nutritional value.

To begin freeze-drying at home, you will need specialized equipment, starting with a home freeze-dryer. Brands like Harvest Right offer models specifically designed for home use, such as the Harvest Right Home Pro Medium. This model can handle 10-15 pounds of food per batch, making it ideal for families and small preppers. Before placing items in the freeze-dryer, pre-freezing is recommended. This step involves freezing the food in a regular freezer to jumpstart the process, reducing the load on the freeze-dryer and ensuring more uniform drying. A vacuum pump is an essential component of the freeze-dryer, creating the low-pressure environment necessary for sublimation. Regular maintenance, such as oil changes for oil-based pumps, is crucial to keep the equipment running efficiently.

Now, let's delve into the specifics of freeze-drying various foods. Fruits like strawberries, apples, and bananas are great candidates for freeze-drying due to their high sugar content, which helps preserve flavor and texture. Begin by washing and slicing the fruits into uniform pieces before pre-freezing them on a baking sheet. Once frozen, transfer the pieces to the freeze-dryer trays, ensuring they are evenly spaced. Vegetables such as peas, corn, and peppers also freeze-dry exceptionally well. Blanch the vegetables briefly to preserve color and texture, then pre-freeze them before placing them in the freeze-dryer. For meats like chicken, beef, and fish, cook them thoroughly before freeze-drying to eliminate any harmful bacteria. Cut the cooked meat into small pieces or strips, pre-freeze, and then arrange them on the trays. The entire freeze-drying process can take anywhere from 24 to 48 hours, depending on the moisture content and thickness of the food.

The benefits of freeze-drying are numerous. The most significant advantage is the long shelf life, with freeze-dried foods lasting up to 25 years when stored properly. This makes them invaluable for emergency preparedness and long-term storage. Nutrient retention is another key benefit. Freeze-drying preserves vitamins, minerals, and beneficial plant compounds better than other drying methods, ensuring that the food remains nutritious. However, it's important to consider the potential drawbacks. The initial cost of a home freeze-dryer can be high, with models like the Harvest Right Home Pro Medium priced around $2,895. Additionally, freeze-drying requires a dedicated space due to the size and weight of the equipment, and it can consume a significant amount of energy. Despite these challenges, the investment in a freeze-dryer can be worthwhile for those committed to maintaining a robust, long-term food supply.

Freeze-drying offers a unique and highly effective way to preserve a wide range of foods. By understanding the science behind the process and investing in the right equipment, you can enjoy the benefits of lightweight, nutrient-rich, and long-lasting preserved foods. Whether you're preparing for an emergency or simply looking to extend the shelf life of your harvest, freeze-drying is a technique that promises both practicality and versatility.

7.2 ROOT CELLARING: NATURAL STORAGE SOLUTIONS

Root cellaring is a time-honored method that utilizes the earth's natural cool and humid conditions to store food. By burying the storage space underground, you harness the insulating power of soil to maintain a stable environment. This insulation keeps temperatures low in the summer and prevents freezing in the winter. Proper ventilation allows for airflow, which is crucial to prevent mold and rot. Seasonal storage of root vegetables and other produce becomes feasible, extending their shelf life significantly. The simplicity of this method lies in its reliance on nature's own cooling systems, making it a sustainable and cost-effective solution for long-term storage.

Constructing or utilizing a root cellar can take various forms. Traditional underground cellars are dug into the ground, often with stone or concrete walls for added insulation. These cellars can be accessed through a stairway or hatch and are ideal for large quantities of produce. Basement root cellars, on the other hand, are built into an existing basement, partitioned off to create a controlled environment. They are convenient since they are close to the living area, making it easy to check on stored items. Outdoor mounds and clamping methods are simpler alternatives. These involve burying vegetables in mounds of soil or straw, often covered with a tarp for added protection. Each method has its own advantages, depending on your space and needs.

Optimizing storage conditions in a root cellar requires attention to detail. Temperature and humidity control are paramount. Aim for temperatures between 32°F and 40°F with a humidity level of

85-95%. Use a thermometer and hygrometer to monitor these conditions regularly. Ventilation is crucial to maintaining airflow and preventing stale air, which can cause spoilage. Create vents at different heights to allow warm air to escape and cool air to enter. Pests can be a problem, so inspect your cellar regularly for signs of rodents or insects. Use natural repellents and ensure that the cellar is sealed well to keep pests out.

Certain types of foods are particularly well-suited for root cellaring. Root vegetables like potatoes, carrots, and beets thrive in the cool, humid environment. Their sturdy nature allows them to last for several months without spoiling. Hardy fruits such as apples and pears can also be stored effectively. They should be kept in crates or bins with good airflow, and it's important to check them regularly for signs of decay. Fermented and canned goods can benefit from the stable conditions of a root cellar, extending their shelf life further. This method offers a way to store a diverse range of foods, making it a versatile addition to your preservation toolkit.

Root cellaring stands out for its simplicity and effectiveness. By leveraging natural elements, you can create a storage solution that is both eco-friendly and efficient. Whether you build a traditional underground cellar, convert a basement space, or use outdoor mounds, the principles remain the same. Control temperature and humidity, ensure proper ventilation, and monitor for pests and spoilage. This method allows you to keep root vegetables, hardy fruits, and preserved goods in prime condition throughout the year. The knowledge of root cellaring connects you to a long tradition of self-sufficiency and resourcefulness, making it a valuable practice for anyone interested in sustainable living.

7.3 VACUUM SEALING FOR EXTENDED SHELF LIFE

Vacuum sealing is one of the most effective methods for extending the shelf life of your preserved foods. By removing air from the packaging, you prevent oxidation, which is the main culprit behind spoilage and nutrient loss. When food is exposed to air, it can degrade and lose its freshness. Vacuum sealing creates an airtight environment that locks in flavor and nutrients, ensuring your food stays as fresh as the day you sealed it. Another significant benefit is the reduction of freezer burn, a common issue when freezing foods. Freezer burn occurs when air reaches the food's surface, causing it to dry out and develop an unappetizing texture. Vacuum sealing eliminates this risk by keeping air out, maintaining the food's quality and texture. Additionally, vacuum sealing offers a compact storage solution, making it easier to organize your pantry or freezer. The packages are typically flat and stackable, allowing you to maximize your storage space efficiently.

When it comes to choosing a vacuum sealer, there are several options to consider. Handheld models are portable and convenient for smaller tasks. They are generally less expensive and take up less space, making them ideal for those with limited kitchen space. However, they may not be as powerful or efficient as countertop models, which are better suited for heavy-duty sealing. Countertop vacuum sealers offer more robust features and can handle larger quantities of food. Within this category, you have external and chamber vacuum sealers. External vacuum sealers are more common and work by sealing the edge of the bag outside the machine. They are versatile and suitable for most home uses. Chamber vacuum sealers, while more expensive, provide a stronger seal and are capable of sealing liquids and moist foods without compromising the seal. They are often used in professional kitchens but can be a worthwhile investment for serious preppers. Additionally, you can choose between automatic and manual sealing functions. Automatic sealers offer the convenience of one-touch operation, while manual sealers give you more control over the sealing process, allowing for custom adjustments.

To vacuum seal various foods effectively, start by preparing your fresh produce. For leafy greens and berries, wash and dry them thoroughly to remove any moisture. Place the produce in a vacuum-seal bag, ensuring it is evenly distributed. Leave enough space at the top of the bag for sealing. Insert the open end of the bag into the vacuum sealer and select the appropriate setting. For delicate items like berries, use the gentle or pulse mode to prevent crushing. When sealing meats and seafood, such as steaks and fish fillets, it's important to pat them dry with a paper towel to remove excess moisture. Place the portions in the vacuum-seal bag, ensuring they lie flat. This not only saves space but also ensures even freezing and thawing. For prepared meals like soups and stews, freeze them in a container first to solidify the liquid, then transfer the frozen block to a vacuum-seal bag. This prevents the liquid from being sucked into the vacuum sealer, ensuring a clean seal.

Maintaining your vacuum sealer is crucial for its longevity and performance. After each use, clean the vacuum sealer thoroughly. Wipe down the exterior with a damp cloth and use a small brush to clean the sealing area and any crevices where food particles might accumulate. For models with detachable parts, wash them in warm, soapy water and let them dry completely before reassembling. Regularly check and replace the gaskets and sealing strips as needed, as worn-out parts can lead to poor seals and air leaks. If you encounter issues like incomplete seals or the machine not sucking air properly, inspect the bags for any punctures or debris that might be interfering with the seal. Keep the vacuum sealer in a cool, dry place when not in use to prevent any damage from humidity or heat. By taking these steps, you ensure that your vacuum sealer remains in top condition, providing you with reliable and effective food preservation for years to come.

7.4 PICKLING BEYOND CUCUMBERS: CREATIVE RECIPES

When we think of pickling, cucumbers often come to mind first. However, advanced pickling techniques open a world of possibilities beyond the humble cucumber. Quick pickling and fermentation pickling offer two distinct methods to preserve and enhance the flavors of a wide variety of vegetables and fruits. Quick pickling involves submerging foods in a vinegar-based brine, which preserves them rapidly, often within a few hours or days. Fermentation pickling, on the other hand, relies on the natural bacteria present on the food to ferment sugars into lactic acid. This method takes longer but results in complex, tangy flavors.

Different types of vinegar and brines can be used to create unique pickling profiles. While white vinegar is a common choice, apple cider vinegar, rice vinegar, and even balsamic vinegar can add interesting nuances. The brine's composition can also vary. Adding sugar can create a sweet and tangy balance, while spices and herbs enhance the overall flavor. Consider incorporating aromatics like garlic, dill, mustard seeds, coriander, and bay leaves to elevate your pickles. For a more adventurous twist, try adding ginger, turmeric, or even chili peppers to your brine for a kick of heat and depth.

Expanding your pickling repertoire starts with exploring diverse recipes. Pickled carrots with ginger and turmeric offer a vibrant, zesty treat that pairs well with salads and sandwiches. Slice the carrots into sticks or coins, and pack them into jars with slivers of fresh ginger and turmeric. Pour a hot brine of apple cider vinegar, water, sugar, and salt over the carrots, seal, and refrigerate. Within a few days, you'll have a delicious, crunchy snack. Spicy pickled radishes are another delightful option. Thinly slice radishes and pack them into jars with garlic and red pepper flakes. A simple brine of white vinegar, water, sugar, and salt transforms these radishes into a tangy, spicy condiment perfect for tacos or burgers. For a sweet and sour twist, try pickling watermelon rind. Peel the green skin and cut the rind into small pieces. Simmer in a brine of vinegar, sugar, water, and spices like cloves and cinnamon. The result is a unique, refreshing pickle that can be enjoyed on its own or as part of a charcuterie board.

Pickling offers several benefits for both flavor and preservation. This method enhances the natural flavors of vegetables and fruits, adding a tangy zest that can elevate any dish. Pickled foods also maintain their crunch and texture, providing a satisfying bite. Besides flavor, pickling extends the shelf life of fresh produce without the need for refrigeration, making it an excellent method for long-term storage. Pickled items can add variety to meals and snacks, serving as side dishes, garnishes, or even main ingredients. A jar of homemade pickles can transform a simple meal, adding complexity and interest.

Safety in pickling is paramount to ensure successful results. Sterilizing jars and equipment is the first step. Boil jars and lids for at least ten minutes to kill any bacteria or mold spores. Monitoring fermentation is crucial, especially when using the fermentation pickling method. Keep an eye on your jars for signs of fermentation, such as bubbles and a sour smell. If you notice mold or an off-putting odor, discard the batch to avoid spoilage. Storing pickled goods in a cool, dark place preserves their quality over time. A pantry or basement shelf works well, but once opened, refrigerate the jars to maintain their freshness and crunch.

Pickling is a versatile and delightful way to preserve a wide variety of foods. By experimenting with different vinegars, brines, and flavorings, you can create unique pickled treats that enhance your meals and snacks. The process is straightforward, yet offers endless possibilities for creativity. Whether you're quick pickling for a fast turnaround or fermenting for complex flavors, pickling brings out the best in your produce, ensuring you enjoy its flavors for months to come.

7.5 PRESERVING WITH MINIMAL EQUIPMENT: PRIMITIVE TECHNIQUES

Exploring traditional and primitive preservation methods can be both fulfilling and practical, especially when modern conveniences aren't available.

Sun and Air Drying

Sun drying and air drying are among the oldest techniques used to preserve food. This method relies on the sun's heat and the natural airflow to remove moisture from the food. To get started, you can build a simple drying rack using materials like wooden frames and fine mesh or cheesecloth. Place the food in a single layer on the rack, ensuring good spacing for air circulation. Position the rack in a sunny, well-ventilated area, turning the food occasionally to promote even drying. Depending on the weather conditions, this process can take several days, but the result is a batch of naturally preserved fruits, vegetables, or herbs.

Smoking Meats

Smoking meats is another age-old method that has stood the test of time. Smoking involves exposing meat to smoke from burning wood or other plant materials, which imparts a rich flavor while preserving the meat. Building a smokehouse or smoker can be a rewarding project. For a simple smoker, you can use a metal drum or an old refrigerator. Create a firebox at the bottom and a smoking chamber above it. Hang the meat in the chamber and light a fire in the firebox, using hardwood like hickory or oak for a flavorful smoke. Maintain a low temperature—around 160°F to 200°F—and smoke the meat for several hours to days, depending on the type and size of the meat.

Curing Meats

Curing meats with salt is another effective primitive technique. Salt draws out moisture and creates an inhospitable environment for bacteria. To prepare salt-cured fish or meats, begin by thoroughly cleaning the meat. Rub it generously with coarse salt, ensuring all surfaces are covered. For an added layer of flavor, mix in herbs and spices like black pepper, garlic, or bay leaves. Place the meat in a non-reactive container and cover it with more salt. Store it in a cool, dry place, turning the meat every few days to ensure even curing. After a few weeks, the meat will be fully cured and ready for storage or consumption.

Primitive preservation methods offer several benefits, including low cost and minimal equipment requirements. You don't need expensive gadgets or electricity, making these techniques highly accessible. However, they also come with challenges. Sun drying and air drying are weather-dependent, requiring consistent heat and low humidity. Smoking and curing meats can be time-consuming and labor-intensive, demanding regular attention and precise control over temperature and humidity. Despite these challenges, the rewards are significant. You gain the ability to preserve food in its most natural form, often with enhanced flavors and textures.

Ensuring safety and success with these primitive methods involves careful monitoring and adherence to best practices. For sun drying and air drying, check the food regularly for signs of spoilage or contamination. Mold or an off smell indicates that the drying process was incomplete or moisture levels were too high. Proper ventilation and airflow are crucial in smoking and curing. Make sure your smokehouse or smoker has adequate ventilation to maintain a consistent smoke flow and prevent creosote buildup, which can impart a bitter taste. Following tested recipes and guidelines for curing and smoking ensures that your preserved meats are safe to eat. These recipes provide precise measurements and instructions, reducing the risk of spoilage or foodborne illnesses.

In this chapter, we've explored various advanced preservation techniques, from freeze-drying and root cellaring to vacuum sealing and creative pickling. Each method offers unique benefits and challenges, contributing to a comprehensive approach to food preservation. As you delve deeper into these techniques, you'll find that the art of preserving food is not only practical but also deeply rewarding. By mastering these methods, you ensure a steady supply of nutritious, flavorful food, regardless of external circumstances.

Next, we'll explore how to ensure consistency and quality in your preservation efforts, diving into the fine details that make a big difference in long-term storage.

CHAPTER 8
ENSURING CONSISTENCY
AND QUALITY

8.1 UNDERSTANDING HEADSPACE AND ITS IMPORTANCE

Headspace in canning is the unfilled space between the top of your food and the lid of the jar. It may seem like a minor detail, but it plays a critical role in the canning process. This space allows for the expansion of food and air during the heating process, ensuring that the jar seals properly as it cools. When jars are heated, the contents expand, and the trapped air is pushed out. As the jars cool, the remaining air contracts, creating a vacuum seal that keeps the contents preserved.

The specific headspace required can vary depending on the type of food you are canning. For high-acid foods, such as fruits and pickles, a headspace of 1/4 to 1/2 inch is typically recommended. This small space is sufficient to allow for the expansion of these foods without compromising the seal. Jams and jellies usually require a headspace of 1/4 inch, which helps in preventing the formation of mold while ensuring a good seal. Low-acid foods, like vegetables and meats, need a larger headspace, generally between 1 to 1 1/4 inches, to accommodate their greater expansion during processing. This extra space is crucial for ensuring a proper vacuum seal and preventing spoilage.

Measuring and adjusting headspace accurately is essential for successful canning. A headspace tool or a simple ruler can help you ensure the correct amount of space is left at the top of the jar. After filling the jar with food, use the tool to measure the distance from the top of the food to the rim of the jar. If necessary, adjust the food levels before sealing. Removing air bubbles is another critical step. Use a non-metallic utensil, such as a plastic knife or a bubble remover, to slide around the inside edges of the jar. This action releases trapped air, which can affect the headspace and the sealing process.

Incorrect headspace can lead to several problems. If too little headspace is left, the food may expand and bubble out during processing. This bubbling can leave deposits on the rim of the jar or the seal of the lid, preventing a proper seal and leading to spoilage. On the other hand, if too much headspace is left, the food at the top is likely to discolor. This is because the extra air in the jar can cause oxidation, affecting the color, taste, and nutritional quality of the food. Moreover, the jar may not seal properly due to insufficient processing time to drive all the air out, leading to potential contamination.

Maintaining the correct headspace is a crucial part of the canning process. By focusing on this important detail, you help ensure that your jars seal correctly, safeguarding the safety and quality of your food. Proper headspace measurement prevents contamination and spoilage while preserving the intended texture and flavor of your canned goods. This careful attention not only preserves your hard work but also guarantees that your pantry is filled with safe and delicious foods, ready to be enjoyed whenever you wish.

8.2 ACHIEVING CONSISTENT RESULTS: TIPS AND TRICKS

Consistency is key when it comes to food preservation, ensuring that each batch you process turns out just as well as the last. One of the most effective strategies for maintaining uniform results is to follow tested recipes precisely. These recipes have been developed and refined to ensure safety and quality, and sticking to them eliminates guesswork. Use standardized measurements and tools to ensure accuracy. Measuring ingredients with a reliable kitchen scale instead of by volume can make a significant difference in the final product. Keeping detailed logs of each preservation session is also invaluable. Record the types of food preserved, the methods used, and any variations in processing times or conditions. This practice not only helps you replicate successful batches but also identifies and corrects any issues that arise.

The quality and uniformity of your ingredients play a crucial role in achieving consistent results. Sourcing high-quality, fresh produce and meats can significantly impact the taste and shelf life of your preserved foods. Fresh ingredients are less likely to harbor bacteria and have better texture and flavor. Ensuring uniform sizes and cuts of ingredients is another important factor. When pieces are of consistent size, they cook and process evenly, preventing some from becoming overcooked while others remain underdone. This uniformity is particularly important in dehydrating and canning, where uneven pieces can lead to inconsistent texture and flavor in the final product.

Controlling processing conditions is essential for consistency. Maintaining consistent temperatures during canning or dehydrating ensures that each jar or piece of food is processed uniformly. Using a reliable thermometer to monitor the temperature of your canning water or dehydrator can help maintain these consistent conditions. For fermentation, monitoring humidity levels is crucial. Too much moisture can lead to mold growth, while too little can cause the food to dry out. Using hygrometers to measure humidity and dehumidifiers or humidifiers to adjust levels can make a significant difference. Accurate timing is another critical factor. Use timers to ensure that each step of the process is performed for the correct duration, preventing under- or over-processing.

Despite best efforts, issues can sometimes arise, and being able to troubleshoot common consistency problems is invaluable. Uneven drying or freezing can be a frequent issue. If you find that your dehydrated foods are not drying evenly, try rotating the trays more frequently or adjusting the slice thickness of your produce.

In freezing, ensure that food is spread out in a single layer during the initial freezing process to prevent clumping. Variations in texture or flavor can also occur. If your canned vegetables are too mushy or your dehydrated fruits lack flavor, consider adjusting the processing times or temperatures. For ensuring even fermentation, regularly check for air bubbles and scum formation, removing any scum that appears to keep the environment ideal for beneficial bacteria.

By following these strategies, you can achieve consistent results in your food preservation efforts. The combination of precise recipes, high-quality ingredients, controlled processing conditions, and effective troubleshooting ensures that each batch of preserved food meets your standards. This attention to detail not only results in better-tasting and longer-lasting preserved foods but also makes the preservation process more predictable and enjoyable.

8.3 QUALITY CONTROL: TESTING AND TASTING PRESERVED FOODS

Ensuring the quality and safety of your preserved foods is a crucial step in the preservation process. Regular testing and tasting are vital to maintain high standards of flavor, texture, and edibility. This practice not only safeguards your health but also guarantees that the effort you put into preserving your harvest yields the best possible results. Quality control involves a series of checks and practices that help you identify and correct any issues before they become significant problems. By incorporating these practices into your routine, you can confidently enjoy your preserved foods, knowing they are both safe and delicious.

Testing your preserved foods begins with a thorough visual inspection. Look for any signs of spoilage, such as discoloration, mold, or unusual cloudiness in liquids. These visual cues can indicate that the food has gone bad and is no longer safe to consume. Smelling the preserved food is another effective way to check for spoilage. Off odors, such as sour, rancid, or musty smells, are clear indicators that the food has spoiled. If any of these signs are present, it is best to discard the food immediately to avoid any risk of foodborne illness. Additionally, tasting small samples can help you assess the flavor and texture. Take a small bite and pay attention to any unusual taste or texture changes, which can signal spoilage or fermentation issues.

Conducting taste tests safely is essential to avoid any health risks. Always use clean utensils when sampling your preserved foods to prevent introducing contaminants. Start by testing small amounts to minimize exposure in case the food is spoiled. Be mindful of any unusual taste or texture changes that could indicate spoilage. If you detect anything off, do not consume the food. Instead, discard it safely and review your preservation process to identify any potential issues. This cautious approach ensures that you can enjoy your preserved foods without compromising your health.

Recording and evaluating the quality of your preserved foods helps you maintain consistent results. Keeping a preservation journal is an excellent way to document your methods and outcomes. Note the types of food preserved, the preservation method used, and any deviations from the expected results. For example, if a batch of canned tomatoes has a different texture than previous batches, record the details and consider any variables that may have affected the outcome. This practice allows you to identify patterns and make necessary adjustments to improve future batches. Additionally, noting the taste and texture of each batch helps you refine your recipes and techniques over time.

Evaluating the quality of your preserved foods involves more than just taste and texture. Consider the overall appearance and presentation of the food. Well-preserved foods should look appetizing and retain their original color and shape as much as possible. Any deviations from this standard can indicate issues with the preservation process. For instance, if your dehydrated fruits appear overly dark or brittle, it may be a sign that they were dried at too high a temperature or for too long. By paying attention to these details, you can ensure that your preserved foods not only taste great but also look appealing.

Adjusting future batches based on your evaluations is a proactive approach to improving your preservation skills. Use the information recorded in your preservation journal to make informed decisions about changes to your methods. For example, if you find that your pickles are consistently too salty, adjust the brine recipe to achieve a better balance. Similarly, if your canned vegetables are too soft, consider reducing the processing time slightly or selecting firmer produce. These adjustments, based on careful evaluation and record-keeping, help you achieve the best possible results with each batch of preserved food.

The importance of quality control in food preservation cannot be overstated. Regular testing and tasting ensure the safety and edibility of your preserved foods, while maintaining high standards of flavor and texture. By incorporating visual inspections, smell tests, and taste tests into your routine, you can confidently enjoy your preserved foods. Recording and evaluating the quality of each batch helps you identify any issues and make necessary adjustments for future batches. This meticulous approach to quality control ensures that your preserved foods are always safe, delicious, and of the highest quality.

8.4 ADJUSTING RECIPES FOR ALTITUDE AND CLIMATE

Altitude can significantly impact food preservation, particularly in canning. As you ascend in altitude, the boiling point of water decreases, meaning it takes less heat for water to boil. This lower boiling point results in less effective processing because the temperatures achieved are insufficient to kill all harmful bacteria and pathogens. Consequently, you need to adjust your canning recipes to ensure safety and effectiveness. For water bath canning, this typically involves adding extra time to the processing. For example, at altitudes of 1,001 to 3,000 feet, you should increase the processing time by five minutes. If you're between 3,001 and 6,000 feet, add ten minutes, and so on.

Pressure canning also requires adjustments. The pressure needs to be increased to compensate for the lower boiling point at higher altitudes. For instance, if you're using a weighted-gauge pressure canner, you should increase the pressure from 10 pounds to 15 pounds for altitudes above 1,000 feet. Dial-gauge canners have more incremental adjustments, but the principle remains the same: higher altitudes necessitate higher pressures. Using altitude charts can help you make these adjustments accurately. These charts provide detailed information on the exact times and pressures needed based on your specific altitude, ensuring your preserved foods are safe to consume.

Climate conditions can also influence preservation methods. Humidity and temperature play crucial roles, especially in dehydrating and fermenting foods. In humid climates, drying times for dehydrated foods can be longer because the air holds more moisture. This added moisture can slow the dehydration process, leading to uneven drying or mold growth. To counteract this, consider using dehumidifiers or fans to reduce the humidity levels in your drying area. These tools help create an environment more conducive to efficient dehydration. On the flip side, if you're in a particularly dry climate, you might need to monitor your foods closely to prevent over-drying, which can make them too brittle.

Fermentation is another method highly sensitive to climate conditions. Warmer temperatures can speed up the fermentation process, sometimes resulting in overly sour or mushy products. Cooler climates can slow down fermentation, requiring longer times to achieve the desired flavor and texture. Using thermostats to monitor and control the temperature can be very helpful. If you live in a warmer climate, you might need to find a cooler spot in your home, like a basement, to ferment your foods. Alternatively, placing your fermentation vessel in a cooler filled with ice packs can help maintain a stable, cool environment. For those in cooler climates, wrapping the vessel in a towel or placing it in a warmer part of the house can help maintain the necessary warmth for fermentation.

Adapting recipes to different climates ensures that you achieve consistent results regardless of where you live. For drying foods in humid conditions, using a dehydrator with adjustable temperature settings can help you fine-tune the drying process. These settings allow you to increase the heat slightly to counteract the humidity without overcooking the food. Monitoring fermentation temperatures with thermostats helps you keep the process under control, preventing the food from fermenting too quickly or too slowly. Storing preserved foods in climate-controlled areas is also essential. Extreme temperatures can affect the shelf life and quality of your preserved foods. A cool, dark pantry or basement is ideal for long-term storage, helping to maintain the integrity of your preserved items.

The impact of altitude and climate on food preservation plays a key role in ensuring the safety and quality of your efforts. By adjusting processing times, pressures, and storage conditions accordingly, you can preserve your foods with confidence, knowing they will remain both safe and delicious. Whether you're facing high altitudes or dealing with extreme humidity, these modifications are essential for achieving optimal results in your food preservation projects.

CHAPTER 9
PRACTICAL STORAGE
SOLUTIONS

9.1 CREATING A PANTRY: ORGANIZING YOUR PRESERVED GOODS

A well-organized pantry is more than just a neat space; it's a vital part of effective food storage. By keeping your pantry orderly, you can significantly reduce food waste. Using older items first ensures that nothing goes to waste, saving you money and resources. This concept is known as the FIFO system, or "First In, First Out." It helps you keep track of what you have and what needs to be used up. An organized pantry also makes meal planning easier. When you can quickly see what's available, planning your weekly meals becomes a breeze. This accessibility ensures you use your preserved foods efficiently, maintaining their quality and safety.

Organizing your preserved goods by category can greatly enhance your pantry's functionality. Grouping items by preservation method—such as canned, dehydrated, frozen, or fermented—allows you to quickly locate what you need. For example, keep all your canned vegetables on one shelf and your dehydrated fruits on another. Further, you can organize by food type. Separate fruits, vegetables, meats, and prepared meals into distinct sections. This method helps you quickly find the specific ingredient you need without rummaging through various jars and containers. Using shelves, bins, and baskets can make this even more efficient. Clear bins allow you to see the contents at a glance, while baskets can hold smaller items that might otherwise get lost.

Optimizing your pantry layout is crucial for maximizing storage and accessibility. Utilize vertical space with adjustable shelving. Shelves that can be moved up or down accommodate jars of different heights and ensure no space is wasted. Keeping frequently used items at eye level ensures you don't have to bend or stretch to reach them, making the pantry more user-friendly. Labeling sections for quick identification also speeds up meal preparation. Clear, readable labels on shelves and bins help you find what you need in seconds. You can even color-code the labels for added convenience, such as using green labels for vegetables and red for fruits.

Examples of effective pantry setups can provide inspiration for your own space. Imagine a pantry with neatly stacked jars of home-canned goods on sturdy, adjustable shelves. Clear plastic bins on lower shelves hold dehydrated foods, while baskets on upper shelves store various kitchen tools. A step-by-step guide to setting up a new pantry can be invaluable. Start by emptying the space completely and giving it a thorough cleaning. Next, install sturdy, adjustable shelving and sort your preserved goods by category. Use clear bins and baskets to keep similar items together. Label each section clearly, and ensure that the heaviest items are stored on lower shelves to prevent accidents. Repurposing existing furniture can also be a clever way to maximize your pantry space. An old bookshelf can be transformed into a storage unit for jars, while a vintage dresser can hold utensils and small kitchen gadgets.

By implementing these practical storage solutions, you can create a pantry that not only looks great but also functions efficiently. An organized pantry reduces food waste, simplifies meal planning, and ensures the safety and quality of your preserved foods. Whether you're new to food preservation or a seasoned pro, taking the time to set up an organized pantry will pay off in the long run, making your preservation efforts even more rewarding.

9.2 INNOVATIVE STORAGE SOLUTIONS FOR SMALL SPACES

In small spaces, every inch counts. Finding creative storage solutions can make a significant difference in how efficiently you can store your preserved foods. One of the most underutilized areas in many homes is the space under the bed. Under-bed storage containers can be a game-changer, allowing you to store jars of canned goods, vacuum-sealed dehydrated foods, or even bags of frozen items. These containers keep your preserved foods out of sight but easily accessible when needed. Installing shelves above doorways is another innovative idea. This often-overlooked space can hold lightweight items like jars of dried herbs or small containers of pickles. Stackable containers and bins are also essential. They maximize vertical space, allowing you to store more in less area. Clear bins are particularly useful as they let you see what's inside at a glance.

Multi-functional furniture can be a lifesaver in small spaces. Look for pieces that serve more than one purpose. Storage ottomans and benches are perfect examples. These can be placed in living areas or bedrooms, providing seating while also offering hidden storage for preserved foods. Kitchen islands with built-in storage are another excellent option. They add valuable counter space for food preparation and come with drawers or shelves underneath for storing jars, containers, and even small appliances. Wall-mounted fold-down tables can be installed in kitchens or pantries. When not in use, they fold up against the wall, saving space. When needed, they provide a sturdy workspace for sorting and organizing your preserved foods.

Maximizing vertical space is crucial in small homes. Installing wall-mounted shelves and racks can create additional storage without taking up floor space. Use these shelves to store jars of canned goods, baskets of dehydrated foods, or even kitchen tools. Over-the-door organizers are another fantastic solution. These can be used on pantry doors, kitchen doors, or even closet doors to hold a variety of items, from jars and containers to bags of dried foods. Hanging pots and pans from ceiling racks frees up cabinet space and keeps your kitchen organized. This method works particularly well in kitchens with high ceilings, utilizing space that would otherwise go unused.

Decluttering is a vital part of maximizing storage space. Regularly purging expired or unused items can free up considerable space. It also ensures that you are only storing what you actually need and will use. Vacuum-sealed bags are excellent for saving space, especially for dried foods and bulk items. They reduce the volume of the items, allowing you to stack and store them more efficiently. Rotating seasonal items in and out of storage can also help you make the most of your available space. Store winter preserves in the summer and vice versa, ensuring that you always have room for your current preservation projects.

Storage Solutions Checklist

- Utilize under-bed storage containers for jars and vacuum-sealed bags.
- Install shelves above doorways for lightweight items.
- Use stackable containers and bins to maximize vertical space.
- Incorporate multi-functional furniture like storage ottomans and kitchen islands with built-in storage.
- Install wall-mounted shelves and racks to create additional storage.
- Use over-the-door organizers for jars and containers.
- Hang pots and pans from ceiling racks to free up cabinet space.
- Regularly purge expired or unused items to free up space.
- Use vacuum-sealed bags to reduce the volume of stored items.
- Rotate seasonal items in and out of storage to make the most of available space.

These innovative storage solutions can transform even the smallest spaces into efficient, organized areas for your preserved foods. By thinking creatively and using every inch of available space, you can ensure that your hard work in preserving food is well-protected and easily accessible.

9.3 LABELING AND TRACKING YOUR PRESERVED FOODS

Proper labeling and tracking of your preserved foods are crucial for preventing waste and ensuring food safety. When you clearly identify the contents and dates on your jars, you avoid the common pitfall of wondering if a jar of pickles is from last summer or two years ago. This clarity helps in keeping track of what you have and prevents overstocking. Over time, it's easy to lose track of what's tucked away in the back of your pantry, especially when you're preserving large quantities of food. By labeling everything accurately, you ensure that older items are used first, maintaining a rotation that keeps your food supply fresh and safe.

Creating effective labels doesn't have to be complicated. Using waterproof markers and durable labels makes sure that the information stays readable even if the jars get wet. Key information to include on each label is the date of preservation, the contents, and the method used. For instance, "Tomato Sauce - 08/21 - Water Bath Canned" provides all the essential details at a glance. Color-coding labels can further simplify the process. Use green labels for vegetables, red for fruits, and blue for meats. This visual cue allows you to quickly identify the type of preserved food, saving time during meal prep.

Tracking inventory is just as important as labeling. Several tools and systems can help you keep an accurate record of your preserved foods. Spreadsheets are a versatile option, allowing you to create detailed logs that can be easily updated. You can include columns for the date, type of food, preservation method, and quantity. Mobile apps designed for pantry management are another excellent choice. These apps often come with features like barcode scanning and expiration reminders, making it easy to keep track of what you have. For those who prefer a more hands-on approach, a handwritten logbook can be just as effective. Maintaining a logbook doesn't require any technology and can be a satisfying way to catalog your efforts.

Setting reminders for expiration checks is a practical way to ensure nothing goes to waste. Whether you use a digital calendar, an app, or a simple wall calendar, regular checks can help you keep tabs on the shelf life of your preserved foods. By scheduling these reminders, you can plan meals around items that are nearing their expiration date, ensuring they are used up in time. This practice not only reduces waste but also ensures that you always have fresh, safe food on hand.

Examples of effective labeling and tracking systems can provide inspiration and guidance. Imagine rows of labeled jars neatly arranged on shelves, each label clearly displaying the contents and date. Printable label templates can simplify the process, offering a uniform look that makes your pantry look organized and professional. Sample inventory tracking sheets can serve as a starting point, helping you set up your own system. These sheets can be as simple or detailed as you need, with sections for different types of preserved foods and spaces for notes on quantities and usage.

By implementing these practices, you can create a system that keeps your preserved foods organized, accessible, and safe. Labeling and tracking might seem like small steps, but they make a significant difference in the efficiency and safety of your food storage. Proper labeling ensures that you always know what you have, while effective tracking helps you avoid overstocking and ensures that older items are used first. Together, these practices help you make the most of your preservation efforts, providing you with a reliable supply of delicious, home-preserved foods.

9.4 UNDERSTANDING SHELF LIFE: HOW LONG DO PRESERVED FOODS LAST?

Understanding the shelf life of various preserved foods is crucial to ensure you consume them safely and enjoy their best quality. Each preservation method offers different longevity. Canned goods typically last between one to two years. This long shelf life makes them a reliable option for long-term storage. The high temperatures used in canning kill bacteria and create a vacuum seal that keeps food safe for extended periods. High-acid foods like fruits and tomatoes tend to last longer than low-acid foods like meats and vegetables. Always check the seals and store them in a cool, dark place to maximize their shelf life.

Dehydrated foods, on the other hand, generally last between six months to a year. The key to extending the shelf life of dehydrated foods is to ensure they are stored in airtight containers to prevent moisture from re-entering. Moisture is the enemy of dehydrated foods, as it can lead to mold and spoilage. Using vacuum-sealed bags or containers with tight-fitting lids can help maintain their dryness. Store these containers in a cool, dark place to keep the food in the best condition. Regularly check for any signs of moisture or spoilage, and use the oldest items first to maintain freshness.

Frozen items have a variable shelf life depending on the type of food. Fruits and vegetables can last up to a year when properly stored, while meats can last six months to a year. The key to preserving frozen foods is to avoid freezer burn, which occurs when air reaches the food's surface and causes it to dry out. Using airtight containers or vacuum-sealed bags can help prevent this.

Labeling with the date of freezing and regularly rotating stock ensures you use older items first. Keep your freezer at 0°F (-18°C) or lower for optimal storage conditions.

Fermented foods can last up to a year if stored properly. The fermentation process creates beneficial bacteria that help preserve the food. However, they need to be kept in a stable environment to maintain their quality. Store fermented foods in a cool, dark place, preferably in glass jars with airtight lids. Regularly check for any signs of spoilage, such as changes in color, texture, or smell. If you notice any mold or off-odors, it's best to discard the food to avoid health risks.

Recognizing signs of spoilage is essential for ensuring that your preserved foods are safe to eat. Changes in color, texture, or smell are the most obvious indicators. For canned goods, look out for gas bubbles or bulging lids, which can signal bacterial growth. If a jar's lid is concave or makes a popping sound when pressed, it has likely lost its seal. Mold or off-odors in dehydrated or fermented foods are clear signs that the food has spoiled. When in doubt, it's always safer to discard questionable items rather than risk consuming spoiled food.

To extend the shelf life of your preserved foods, store them in cool, dark places. Excessive heat or light can degrade the quality of preserved foods and shorten their shelf life. Using airtight containers is another effective strategy. Containers with tight-fitting lids or vacuum-sealed bags prevent moisture and air from reaching the food, which helps maintain its quality. Regularly rotating your stock is essential. Using older items first ensures that nothing goes to waste and that you always have the freshest preserved foods available. Keeping an inventory and updating it regularly can help you stay on top of your food supply, making it easier to plan meals and avoid overstocking.

9.5 EMERGENCY PREPAREDNESS: BUILDING A RELIABLE FOOD SUPPLY

In today's unpredictable world, having a reliable food supply is not just a good idea; it's a necessity. Natural disasters, economic instability, and global supply chain disruptions can all impact our access to food. By preparing a well-stocked emergency food supply, you ensure food security for you and your family, providing peace of mind in uncertain times. This reduces dependency on external food sources, which can be unreliable during crises. Knowing that you have a reserve of food can alleviate anxiety and give you the confidence to face emergencies head-on.

Building an emergency food supply starts with the basics. Begin by creating a three-day supply of non-perishable foods, which can sustain you through short-term disruptions. Focus on nutrient-dense items that provide a balanced diet, such as canned beans, dried fruits, and whole grains. Once you have a three-day supply, gradually build up to several months. This incremental approach makes the task less overwhelming and more manageable. Diversify your stockpile with a variety of preservation methods. Include canned goods for their long shelf life, dehydrated foods for their compact storage, and frozen items for their convenience. Fermented foods can also be a valuable addition, offering both nutrition and probiotic benefits.

Preserved foods play a crucial role in emergency preparedness. Their shelf-stable nature makes them easy to store and manage. Unlike fresh produce, which can spoil quickly, preserved foods can last for months or even years. This longevity ensures that you always have access to nutritious meals, regardless of external circumstances. The versatility of preserved foods also simplifies meal preparation. With a well-stocked pantry, you can easily create a variety of dishes using the ingredients at hand. High nutritional value is another significant benefit. Home-preserved foods retain most of their vitamins and minerals, providing essential nutrients that support health and well-being during stressful times.

Maintaining and rotating your emergency food supply is essential for keeping it fresh and ready to use. Regularly check expiration dates to ensure that none of your preserved foods go to waste. This habit also helps you identify which items need to be used first. Rotating your stock is a straightforward way to keep your supply fresh. When you add new items, place them at the back of the shelf and move older items to the front. This practice ensures that you are always using the oldest items first, maintaining a continuous cycle of fresh food. Keeping an inventory and updating it regularly can simplify this process. A well-maintained inventory helps you track what you have, what you need, and when items are approaching their expiration dates.

A reliable food supply is more than just a collection of preserved foods; it's a lifeline during emergencies. By following these guidelines, you can create a stockpile that not only sustains you through difficult times but also provides peace of mind. Regular maintenance and rotation ensure that your food supply remains fresh and nutritious, ready to support you whenever needed. Building a reliable food supply is an ongoing process, but the benefits far outweigh the effort.

CHAPTER 10
RECIPES AND MEAL PLANNING WITH PRESERVED FOODS

This chapter is dedicated to showing you how meals in a jar can bring ease and variety to your daily routine, all while ensuring you make the most of your preserved foods.

10.1 MEALS IN A JAR: CONVENIENT AND NUTRITIOUS OPTIONS

Meals in a jar are a brilliant solution for anyone looking to simplify meal prep without sacrificing nutrition. These pre-portioned meals can be assembled in advance, making them perfect for busy mornings, quick lunches, or effortless dinners. The concept is simple: layer ingredients in mason jars or similar containers, seal them up, and store them until you're ready to eat. This method not only saves time but also ensures that your meals are well-balanced and tailored to your dietary needs.

Layering ingredients is key to successful meals in a jar. For breakfast jars, start with a base like oats or yogurt, followed by layers of fruits, nuts, and seeds. This not only creates a visually appealing meal but also keeps ingredients fresh and flavorful. For salads, begin with the dressing at the bottom, followed by hearty vegetables like cucumbers and tomatoes, then lighter greens on top. This prevents sogginess and ensures that everything stays crisp. Soups and stews can be layered with grains or pasta at the bottom, canned meats or beans in the middle, and vegetables on top. When you're ready to eat, simply add water or broth, heat, and enjoy.

The portability of mason jars makes them ideal for meals on the go. Whether you're heading to work, school, or a day out in the wilderness, these jars can be easily packed and transported. They are also highly customizable. You can adjust the ingredients to suit your dietary preferences, whether you're vegetarian, gluten-free, or following a specific eating plan. This flexibility makes meals in a jar a versatile option for anyone looking to maintain a healthy diet while managing a busy schedule.

Let's explore a few recipes to get you started. For breakfast, try overnight oats with dehydrated fruits and nuts. In a mason jar, combine rolled oats, chia seeds, and a bit of sweetener like honey or maple syrup. Top with a mix of your favorite dehydrated fruits —think apples, berries, or bananas—and a handful of nuts. Add milk or a dairy-free alternative, seal the jar, and refrigerate overnight. In the morning, you'll have a delicious, nutritious breakfast ready to go.

For lunch, mason jar salads are a fantastic option. Start with a layer of your favorite dressing, followed by sturdy vegetables like cherry tomatoes, bell peppers, and cucumbers. Add a layer of preserved vegetables, such as pickled beets or carrots, for extra flavor. Top with greens like spinach or arugula, and finish with a protein source like canned chickpeas or grilled chicken. Seal the jar and store it in the fridge until you're ready to eat. When lunchtime rolls around, simply shake the jar to mix the ingredients and enjoy a fresh, vibrant salad.

Dinner can be just as effortless with soups and stews using canned meats and vegetables. For a hearty chicken noodle soup, layer cooked pasta at the bottom of a jar, followed by canned chicken, preserved carrots, and celery. Add some herbs and spices for flavor, seal the jar, and store it in the fridge. When you're ready to eat, pour the contents into a pot, add broth, and heat until warm. This method ensures you always have a comforting, homemade meal ready in minutes.

Meals in a jar offer numerous benefits for busy lifestyles. They are quick and easy to prepare, often taking just a few minutes of assembly time. This makes them perfect for meal prep on week-ends, ensuring you have nutritious options ready throughout the week. These meals are also well-balanced, providing a mix of proteins, carbs, and fats to keep you energized and satisfied. By controlling portion sizes, they help reduce food waste and prevent overeating, making them a smart choice for anyone looking to maintain a healthy diet.

To assemble and store meals in a jar effectively, consider a few key tips. Using vacuum-sealed jars can extend the freshness of your ingredients, especially for salads and other perishable items. This method removes air from the jar, preventing spoilage and keeping your meals crisp and delicious. Layering ingredients strategically is also crucial. For example, placing dressings and wet ingredients at the bottom of salad jars prevents greens from becoming soggy. Similarly, keeping dried ingredients separate until ready to eat can maintain their texture and flavor.

Storing meals in the refrigerator or freezer ensures they stay fresh and ready to grab when you need them. Breakfast jars like overnight oats can be stored in the fridge for up to five days, while salads typically last three to four days. Soups and stews can be frozen for longer storage, often up to several months. Just be sure to leave some headspace in the jars to allow for expansion during freezing.

Incorporating meals in a jar into your routine can revolutionize the way you approach meal prep and daily nutrition. These convenient, nutritious options make it easy to enjoy home-cooked meals without the hassle of daily cooking. By taking a little time to prepare these jars in advance, you ensure that you always have a healthy, delicious meal at your fingertips, no matter how busy life gets.

10.2 GOURMET RECIPES WITH PRESERVED INGREDIENTS

When it comes to elevating your home-cooked meals, incorporating preserved ingredients can transform simple dishes into gourmet experiences.

Braised Short Ribs

Imagine the rich, savory taste of braised short ribs enhanced by the depth of pressure-canned vegetables. This dish not only showcases the versatility of preserved foods but also highlights the importance of quality ingredients in gourmet cooking. Start by gathering your ingredients: 4 pounds of beef short ribs, 2 cups of pressure-canned carrots, 1 cup of pressure-canned pearl onions, and a mix of fresh herbs like rosemary and thyme. Season the short ribs with salt and pepper, then sear them in a hot skillet until they're browned on all sides. Transfer the ribs to a slow cooker, adding the canned vegetables and a cup of beef broth. Let everything cook on low for 6-8 hours until the meat is tender and the flavors meld together. Serve the ribs over a bed of creamy mashed potatoes, garnished with a sprig of fresh rosemary for an elegant touch.

Mushroom Risotto

Another dish that benefits immensely from preserved ingredients is dehydrated mushroom risotto. The earthy flavor of mushrooms, when preserved through dehydration, intensifies and adds a gourmet twist to this classic Italian dish. To prepare, you'll need 1 cup of arborio rice, 1/2 cup of dehydrated mushrooms, 1 small onion finely chopped, and 4 cups of chicken stock. Begin by rehydrating the mushrooms in warm water for about 20 minutes. In a large pan, sauté the onions in olive oil until they're translucent. Add the arborio rice and stir to coat each grain with oil. Slowly add the chicken stock, one ladle at a time, allowing the rice to absorb the liquid before adding more. Stir in the rehydrated mushrooms and their soaking liquid for an extra boost of flavor. Continue cooking until the rice is creamy and tender. Finish with a generous handful of grated Parmesan cheese and a drizzle of truffle oil, if you have it on hand, for a truly luxurious meal.

Fermented Kimchi Fried Rice

For those who enjoy a bit of spice and complexity, fermented kimchi fried rice is a must-try. This dish is a fantastic way to use homemade kimchi, offering a balance of tangy, spicy, and umami flavors. Gather 2 cups of cooked and cooled rice, 1 cup of fermented kimchi, 1 small carrot julienned, 1 small zucchini diced, and 2 eggs. Heat a large skillet or wok over medium-high heat and add a tablespoon of sesame oil. Sauté the carrots and zucchini until they're tender, then push them to the side of the pan. Crack the eggs into the empty space and scramble until just set. Add the rice and kimchi, stirring everything together until heated through. Season with a splash of soy sauce and a sprinkle of toasted sesame seeds. Serve hot, garnished with chopped green onions and a fried egg on top for an extra layer of flavor.

The quality of your preserved ingredients plays a significant role in the success of these gourmet dishes. Using premium meats and fresh produce for canning ensures that the flavors remain vibrant and delicious. Proper seasoning and brining techniques are also crucial. For example, a well-seasoned brine for your pressure-canned vegetables can enhance their taste and texture, making them a perfect complement to rich meats like short ribs. Balancing flavors is another key aspect. Combining the intense flavors of preserved ingredients with fresh ones creates a harmonious and dynamic meal. For instance, pairing the bright acidity of canned tomatoes with the freshness of basil in a pasta sauce can elevate a simple dish to something special.

When it comes to pairing preserved foods with fresh ingredients, the possibilities are endless. Canned tomatoes, for example, are a pantry staple that can be used in countless recipes. Combine them with fresh herbs like basil and oregano to create a quick and flavorful marinara sauce. Sauté some garlic in olive oil, add the canned tomatoes, and let it simmer for 20 minutes. Stir in the fresh herbs just before serving over pasta for a simple yet sophisticated meal. Dehydrated vegetables can also add a unique twist to fresh salads. Rehydrate them by soaking in warm water for a few minutes, then toss them with fresh greens, cherry tomatoes, and a tangy vinaigrette. The combination of textures and flavors makes for a delightful and nutritious salad.

Fermented pickles are another versatile ingredient that can be paired with fresh foods to create balanced and flavorful meals. They add a crunchy, tangy element that complements rich and savory dishes. For example, serve a charcuterie board with a variety of cured meats, cheeses, and fermented pickles. The acidity of the pickles cuts through the richness of the meats and cheeses, creating a well-rounded and satisfying appetizer. Another idea is to use fermented pickles as a topping for sandwiches and burgers. The bright, zesty flavor adds a refreshing contrast to the hearty proteins and creamy condiments.

Incorporating preserved ingredients into your gourmet cooking not only enhances the flavors of your dishes but also showcases the versatility and convenience of food preservation. By combining preserved and fresh ingredients thoughtfully, you can create meals that are both delicious and dynamic. Whether you're preparing a sophisticated dinner for guests or a simple meal for your family, the use of high-quality preserved foods can elevate your cooking to new heights.

10.3 MEAL PLANNING FOR BUSY WEEKNIGHTS: QUICK AND EASY IDEAS

Efficient meal planning can be a game-changer, especially when you leverage the power of preserved foods. The first step is prepping ingredients in advance. By chopping vegetables, marinating meats, and portioning out grains on a weekend, you save valuable minutes on weeknights. For instance, you can pre-slice bell peppers and onions, store them in airtight containers, and have them ready for a quick stir-fry. Similarly, marinating chicken in a vacuum-sealed bag and freezing it ensures that you have flavorful, ready-to-cook protein whenever you need it.

Using preserved foods to cut down on cooking time is another effective strategy. Canned tomatoes, for example, can be a lifesaver. Instead of simmering fresh tomatoes for hours, you can open a jar of your home-canned batch and have a rich sauce ready in minutes. Dehydrated vegetables, once rehydrated, cook much faster than fresh ones, making them ideal for quick meals. Imagine tossing rehydrated mushrooms into a hot pan with some garlic and olive oil—they'll cook up in no time, adding depth to your dish without the lengthy prep.

Creating a weekly meal plan that incorporates these preserved staples can streamline your weeknight dinners. Start by planning out your meals for the week, considering what you already have in your pantry. Knowing that you have canned beans, pickled jalapeños, and frozen meats on hand can inspire a variety of dishes. For example, Monday could feature a hearty one-pot pasta with canned tomatoes and vegetables. Tuesday might be a quick stir-fry with dehydrated veggies and frozen chicken. Wednesday could be taco night, using canned beans and pickled jalapeños for a zesty kick. By planning ahead, you not only save time but also reduce the stress of figuring out what to cook each night.

For practical and delicious weeknight meals, consider these quick and easy recipe ideas.

Pasta with Tomatoes and Vegetables

A one-pot pasta with canned tomatoes and vegetables is a perfect example. Start by sautéing some garlic and onions in olive oil. Add a jar of canned tomatoes, a handful of dehydrated spinach (rehydrated in a bit of hot water), and your choice of pasta. Add enough water or broth to cover the pasta, bring it to a boil, then simmer until the pasta is cooked and the sauce is thickened. This dish requires minimal cleanup and delivers maximum flavor.

Chicken and Vegetable Stir Fry

Stir-fries are another fantastic option. Use your pre-prepped veggies and frozen meats for a speedy dinner. Heat some oil in a large skillet or wok and add your rehydrated vegetables. Once they're tender, push them to the side and add your frozen, pre-marinated chicken. Stir everything together, add a splash of soy sauce or your favorite stir-fry sauce, and serve over rice or noodles. This method allows you to have a nutritious, homemade meal on the table in under 30 minutes.

Tacos with Beans and Jalapenos

Tacos with canned beans and pickled jalapeños are a go-to for busy nights. Warm up some tortillas and heat a can of beans with a bit of cumin and chili powder. Top the beans with shredded cheese, pickled jalapeños, and any other toppings you enjoy, such as lettuce, tomatoes, or avocado. This meal is not only quick and easy but also highly customizable to suit everyone's taste.

Using preserved foods for weeknight meals offers several benefits. First, it reduces your reliance on takeout and processed foods, which are often less nutritious and more expensive. By using ingredients you've preserved yourself, you know exactly what's in your food, avoiding unwanted additives and preservatives. Second, it saves money. Home-preserved foods are often more affordable than fresh or commercially preserved options. You can buy in bulk when produce is in season and prices are lower, then preserve it for use throughout the year. Finally, it minimizes food waste. By preserving surplus produce and incorporating it into your meal plan, you make the most of what you have and reduce the amount of food that goes to waste.

Batch cooking and freezing meals can further enhance your efficiency. Cooking large batches of soups and stews, for example, allows you to have multiple meals ready to go. Simply portion them into freezer-safe containers or vacuum-sealed bags, label them with the date and contents, and freeze. When you need a quick dinner, just thaw and reheat. This method is particularly useful for those nights when you're too tired to cook from scratch.

Using vacuum-sealed bags for portioned meals can keep your freezer organized and your meals fresh. Divide large batches of cooked food into single or family-sized portions, seal them, and store them flat to save space. Labeling and dating your frozen meals is crucial for easy rotation. By knowing what you have and when it was preserved, you can ensure you're using the oldest items first, keeping your stock fresh and reducing waste.

Efficient meal planning with preserved foods can significantly simplify your weeknight dinners. By prepping ingredients in advance, using preserved staples to cut down on cooking time, and creating a weekly meal plan, you can streamline your cooking process. Quick and easy recipes like one-pot pasta, stir-fries, and tacos make dinner preparation a breeze. The benefits of using preserved foods extend beyond convenience; they also offer cost savings and minimize food waste. Batch cooking and freezing meals further enhance your efficiency, ensuring you always have nutritious, home-cooked meals ready to go.

CONCLUSION

As we reach the end of "The Preserver's Handbook," I want to take a moment to reflect on why this book was written. It serves as a comprehensive guide designed to empower you with the knowledge and skills needed for canning, preserving, fermenting, freezing, and dehydrating foods for long-term storage. The goal has always been to help you achieve greater self-sufficiency, prepare for emergencies, save money, and ensure you have access to healthier, preservative-free foods.

Throughout the chapters, we explored various methods of food preservation, starting with the basics and moving toward more advanced techniques.

In **Chapter 1**, we discussed the importance of food preservation in modern times, including self-sufficiency, preparedness, cost savings, and health benefits. We covered the essential tools and equipment you'll need, along with basic safety principles to avoid spoilage and contamination.

Chapter 2 introduced you to water bath canning, ideal for high-acid foods like fruits, jams, and pickles. We walked through the step-by-step process, from preparing food and jars to ensuring a successful seal and proper storage.

In **Chapter 3**, we ventured into pressure canning, which is necessary for preserving low-acid foods like vegetables, meats, and soups. We detailed the equipment needed, the process, and troubleshooting tips to ensure your efforts are successful and safe.

Chapter 4 delved into dehydrating fruits and vegetables, highlighting the benefits of this method, such as lightweight and compact storage, long shelf life, and nutritional retention. We discussed how to choose the right dehydrator, prepare produce for drying, and store and use dehydrated foods.

Chapter 5 focused on fermenting for flavor and health. We explored the science behind fermentation, essential equipment, and step-by-step guides for fermenting vegetables and making sauerkraut and kimchi. We also tackled common fermentation problems and solutions.

Chapter 6 covered freezing for long-term storage, emphasizing the simplicity and effectiveness of this method. We provided guidelines for preparing foods for freezing, best practices for freezing fruits and vegetables, and step-by-step instructions for freezing meats and seafood.

Chapter 7 introduced advanced preservation techniques like freeze-drying, root cellaring, and vacuum sealing. We explored the equipment needed, benefits, and potential drawbacks of each method, along with practical tips for success.

Chapter 8 highlighted the importance of ensuring consistency and quality in your preservation efforts. We discussed headspace, strategies for uniformity, quality control, adjusting recipes for altitude and climate.

Chapter 9 focused on practical storage solutions, from creating an organized pantry to innovative storage ideas for small spaces. We also covered labeling, tracking, understanding shelf life, and building a reliable food supply for emergency preparedness.

In **Chapter 10**, we provided recipes and meal planning ideas using preserved foods. We explored meals in a jar, gourmet recipes with preserved ingredients, and quick and easy weeknight meal ideas.

The key takeaways from this book are clear: food preservation is a valuable skill that offers numerous benefits, from self-sufficiency and cost savings to improved health and preparedness. With the right tools, knowledge, and practice, anyone can successfully preserve their own food.

I understand that starting or continuing your food preservation journey might seem daunting. But remember, every expert was once a beginner. With practice, you'll gain confidence and proficiency. The benefits of preserving your own food—knowing exactly what's in your meals, reducing waste, and enjoying the taste of homegrown produce year-round—are well worth the effort.

Now, I encourage you to take immediate steps to start or expand your food preservation efforts. Try a simple recipe like canning your favorite jam or dehydrating apple slices. Invest in essential equipment, like a pressure canner or a dehydrator, if you haven't already. Consider joining a local food preservation group or an online community to connect with others who share your interests.

Thank you for choosing this book and trusting in the guidance provided. Your commitment to self-sufficiency, health, and sustainability is commendable. I'm grateful for the opportunity to share my knowledge and experiences with you, and I hope this book has been a valuable resource on your journey.

I invite you to share your experiences, successes, and challenges. Join online communities or follow social media pages dedicated to food preservation. By sharing your journey, you can inspire and learn from others, fostering a supportive and knowledgeable community.

As a final thought, I'd like to leave you with a quote that has always resonated with me: "The greatest wealth is health." By preserving your own food, you're not just preparing for the future—you're investing in the health and well-being of yourself and your loved ones.

Happy preserving!

-The Grinning Gardener

REFERENCES

Food preservation | Definition, Importance, Methods. (n.d.). *Encyclopedia Britannica*. https://www.britannica.com/topic/food-preservation

Essential tools for canning guide. (n.d.). *The Prairie Farm Table*. https://theprairie farmtable.com/essential-tools-for-canning/

USDA's complete guide to home canning. (n.d.). *USDA National Institute of Food and Agriculture*. https://www.nifa.usda.gov/about-nifa/blogs/usdas-complete-guide-home-canning

Effective strategies for sourcing local ingredients. (n.d.). *Auguste Escoffier School of Culinary Arts*. https://www.escoffier.edu/blog/culinary-arts/effective-strate gies-for-sourcing-local-ingredients/

Water bath canning. (n.d.). *Ball Mason Jars*. https://www.ballmasonjars.com/water-bath-canning.html

High-acid foods - Canning. (n.d.). *University of California Agriculture and Natural Resources*. https://ucanr.edu/sites/inyomonomfp/ Safe_Food_Preservation/Canning/High-Acid_Foods/

The 6 best canning jars | Tested & rated. (n.d.). *Tech Gear Lab*. https://www.techgearlab.com/topics/kitchen/best-canning-jars

Common canning mistakes and how to avoid them. (n.d.). *The Spruce Eats*. https://www.thespruceeats.com/how-to-avoid-common-canning-mistakes-1327444

Principles of home canning. (n.d.). *National Center for Home Food Preservation*. https://nchfp.uga.edu/papers/guide/GUIDE01_HomeCan_rev0715.pdf

USDA's complete guide to home canning. (n.d.). *USDA National Institute of Food and Agriculture*. https://www.nifa.usda.gov/about-nifa/blogs/usdas-complete-guide-home-canning

Pressure canners: Dial gauge or weighted gauge? (n.d.). *Healthy Canning*. https://www.healthycanning.com/pressure-canners-dial-gauge-or-weighted-gauge

Under pressure: Pressure canning for advanced preserving. (n.d.). *The Chopping Block*. https://www.thechoppingblock.com/blog/under-pressure-pressure-canning-for-advanced-preserving

The 4 best food dehydrators, according to our tests. (n.d.). *Food & Wine*. https://www.foodandwine.com/lifestyle/kitchen/best-food-dehydrators

How to dehydrate fruits and vegetables for a healthy snack. (n.d.). *Eating Well*. https://www.eatingwell.com/article/290910/how-to-dehydrate-fruits-and-vegetables-for-a-healthy-snack/

Dehydrating food: Is it good for you? (n.d.). *WebMD*. https://www.webmd.com/diet/dehydrating-food-good-for-you.

Let's preserve: Drying fruits and vegetables (dehydration). (n.d.). *Penn State Extension*. https://extension.psu.edu/lets-preserve-drying-fruits-and-vegetables-dehydration.

The science of lactic acid fermentation. (n.d.). *Serious Eats*. https://www.seriouseats.com/science-of-lactic-acid-fermentation-preservation

8 surprising benefits of sauerkraut (plus how to make it). (n.d.). *Healthline*. https://www.healthline.com/nutrition/benefits-of-sauerkraut

Beginners guide to fermentation: Essential tools. (n.d.). *Revolve Primal Health*. https://www.revolveprimalhealth.com/blog/beginners-guide-to-fermentation-essential-tools/

Fermented vegetables troubleshooting FAQ. (n.d.). *Cultures for Health*. https://culturesforhealth.com/blogs/learn/natural-fermentation-fermented-vegetables-troubleshooting-faq

Freezing food as a food preservation method, pros and cons. (n.d.). *Sage Urban Homesteading*. https://www.sage-urban-homesteading.com/freezing-food.html

Blanching and freezing vegetables. (n.d.). *University of Illinois Extension*. https://extension.illinois.edu/food/blanching-and-freezing-vegetables

How should food be packaged for the freezer? (n.d.). *Ask USDA*. https://ask.usda.gov/s/article/How-should-food-be-packaged-for-the-freezer.

Freezing and food safety. (n.d.). *U.S. Department of Agriculture*. http://www.fsis.usda.gov/food-safety/safe-food-handling-and-preparation/food-safety-basics/freezing-and-food-safety

Freeze drying: How it works, benefits, and how-to. (n.d.). *Healthline*. https://www.healthline.com/nutrition/freeze-drying

Best freeze dryer for home freeze drying. (n.d.). *True Prepper*. https://trueprepper.com/best-freeze-dryer/

How to build a root cellar: A step-by-step guide. (n.d.). *GroCycle*. https://grocycle.com/how-to-build-a-root-cellar/

The benefits of vacuum sealing for long-term food storage. (n.d.). *Fresh Farms*. https://www.freshfarms.com/the-benefits-of-vacuum-sealing-for-long-term-food-storage/

Watch the headspace. (n.d.). *Clemson University*. https://www.clemson.edu/extension/food/canning/canning-tips/09headspace.html.

Quality control in the food industry: A guide. (n.d.). *TDI PackSys*. https://www.tdipacksys.com/blog/quality-control-in-the-food-industry/

Altitude adjustments for home canning. (n.d.). *South Dakota State University Extension*. https://extension.sdstate.edu/altitude-adjustments-home-canning

Recipes using my preserved food. (n.d.). *Stoney Creek Farm.* https://stoneycreek
farmtennessee.com/recipes-using-my-preserved-food/

Organizing a prepared pantry: Everyday and bulk pantry storage. (n.d.). *Silo &
Sage.* https://siloandsage.com/2021/11/17/organizing-a-prepared-pantry-
everyday-and-bulk-pantry-storage/

18 creative storage ideas for small spaces to get organized. (n.d.). *Better Homes &
Gardens.* https://www.bhg.com/decorating/small-spaces/strategies/creative-
storage-ideas-for-small-spaces/

The best practices in food traceability. (n.d.). *Lowry Solutions.* https://lowrysolu
tions.com/blog/the-best-practices-in-food-traceability/

Packaging and storing dried foods. (n.d.). *National Center for Home Food
Preservation.* https://nchfp.uga.edu/how/dry/drying-general/packaging-and-
storing-dried-foods/

Eight great meal in a jar recipes. (n.d.). *Make-Ahead Meal Mom.* https://www.makea
headmealmom.com/eight-great-meal-jar-recipes/

Top 15 advantages to vacuum sealing your food. (n.d.). *VacMaster.* https://www.
vacmasterfresh.com/fresh-bites-blog/top-15-advantages-to-vacuum-sealing-
your-food/?srsltid=
AfmBOorXPFIcVcBQvn8WfL9DE95tb1VKRQ0LD8bGBZnqMC
Qt3OSkoCmw

97 super simple recipes made with canned foods. (n.d.). *Taste of Home.* https://
www.tasteofhome.com/collection/recipes-made-canned-foods/

Home food preservation: Preserving plan for a year's worth of food. (n.d.). *Melissa
K. Norris.* https://melissaknorris.com/podcast/home-food-preservation-
preserving-plan-for-a-years-worth-of-food/

AUTHOR BIO

Kent Jameson grew up in a small farm town in Iowa, where he developed a deep appreciation for the simplicity of rural life. In 1994, he earned a Bachelor of Science degree in Family and Consumer Sciences Journalism from Iowa State University, laying the foundation for a life dedicated to exploring the intersection of family, health, and everyday issues that confront people.

Passionate about natural health, alternative medicines, and sustainable living, Kent's writing focuses on issues that directly affect families and consumers, offering thoughtful insights into how people can live healthier, more balanced lives in today's fast-paced world. Whether he's exploring the benefits of organic gardening, promoting holistic wellness practices, or discussing the challenges of modern life, Kent's work is always grounded in practical, real-world experience.

When he's not writing or tending to his garden, Kent enjoys spending time with his two sons, often cheering them on from the sidelines as they play basketball. Currently residing in Phoenix, Arizona, he continues to live by the values of simplicity and wellness that have guided him throughout his life and career.